From Fantasyland To The Rat Race

A Practical Guide to Thriving in the Real World

by
Scott M. O'Neil and Eric J. Hinds

authorHOUSE™

1663 LIBERTY DRIVE, SUITE 200
BLOOMINGTON, INDIANA 47403
(800) 839-8640
WWW.AUTHORHOUSE.COM

First published by AuthorHouse 12/15/04

ISBN: 1-4208-1994-1 (sc)

Printed in the United States of America
Bloomington, Indiana

This book is printed on acid-free paper.

ADVANCE PRAISE

"Successful business people don't start at the top. Every great business leader has had to make the leap from the DREAMS of childhood to the harsh realities of adulthood and the 'rat race.' 'From Fantasy Land to the Rat Race' provides life lessons that will save future leaders from making the common mistakes that stall a career. You must read this book, internalize it, know it … then read it again."

— Len Komoroski
President, Cleveland Cavaliers/Gund Arena

"When reading this book, I thought of the lumps and whacks I took in building the first blocks of my career. If you read this book, you'll get the career you want quicker and faster and without any lumps or whacks."   — Jon Spoelstra
President, Mandalay Baseball Properties

"'From Fantasy Land to the Rat Race' provides life lessons that will save future leaders from falling off a cliff. I should have read it years ago. You must read this book, and then read it again."   — Seth Berger
CEO, And 1

"Everyone always tells you that you have to 'hustle, network, get a mentor, etc.,' in order to get ahead in business. But funny that no one ever tells you HOW to do any of these things. Finally here's a book that not only explains in detail how to get into AND ahead in the work force, but provides real examples — the good, the bad, and the ugly — of how a number of successful business people did it themselves. If you're graduating from college or just starting to work, this book is a must read. 'Rat Race' will save you from saying, like I did, 'If I'd only known then what I know now.'"

— Toby Shorter, President, A Touch of Jazz, Inc.
(Music production company/label; producers of music
for Will Smith, Jill Scott, Musiq, Lil' Kim)

"For the young professional, the road to success is often times a maze filled with a lot of potholes, dead ends and traffic jams. Your road to success will not be the same as your friend's. Scott and Eric provide the tools to identify your individual highway to success and the insights necessary to travel that road. Quickly. Professionally. Successfully. Ten years down the road don't be the one saying, 'I should have read … Fantasy Land.'"   — Dr. Greg Bonner
Marketing Department Chair, Villanova University

Eric J. Hinds grew up in Middletown, N.J. Eric graduated from Villanova in 1992 with a major in marketing, where he played varsity soccer and was president of the Marketing Society. Eric accepted a position in March 1993 with Automatic Data Processing as an entry-level sales representative. He quickly established himself as a top sales person finishing among the top three in sales in the entire region. A regular at the annual President's Club trips, Eric was ranked number five in the nation out of 1,700 sales reps across the country. In January 1996, Eric was promoted to sales manager. He was the youngest sales manager in the history of the region and built a reputation as an up-and-coming manager. Eric's teams continually exceeded their goals and finished each year at the top of the heap. In July 1997, Eric was promoted to sales director and was instrumental in developing and creating new and innovative revenue streams. Eric decided to join a large brokerage house in May 1998 as an assistant vice president. Eric currently lives in Holmdel, N.J., with his wife Karen and two sons Eric and Connor.

Scott M. O'Neil grew up in Newburgh, N.Y. Scott graduated with honors from Villanova in 1992. Hired by the New Jersey Nets as the corporate marketing assistant in August 1992, O'Neil became proficient in making coffee, ordering lunch and typing memos. Seven months later he was promoted to corporate marketing manager, a position in which he was responsible for selling corporate sponsorships. In December 1994, at age 24, O'Neil accepted the position of director, corporate sales for the Philadelphia Eagles, becoming the youngest director in the NFL. In this capacity, he was responsible for managing and growing the sponsorship and promotions department. He left in 1997 to attend Harvard Business School, where he was awarded his M.B.A. in June 1998. While at HBS, Scott was selected by his classmates to represent the class by speaking at graduation. He returned to the Eagles in June 1998, to accept the position of vice president, sales — at age 28 becoming the youngest vice president in the league, where he oversaw a $40 million budget of tickets, suites and hospitality. After a quick stab at Internet millions as president of HoopsTV.com, Scott accepted a position as vice president of team marketing at the National Basketball Association. Scott currently resides in Rosemont, Penn., with his wife Lisa and daughters Alexa and Kira.

DEDICATION

To my wife and love of my life, Lisa, and my daughters
Alexa and Kira, girls who changed the way I see the world.
— Scott M. O'Neil

To my wife Karen, my sons Eric and Connor …
Everything I do is for them!
— Eric J. Hinds

ACKNOWLEDGMENTS

A special thanks to our friends, co-workers and associates who contributed their time, stories and anecdotes that make this book a more interesting and practical read.

EJH. After nearly five years of on-and-off writing, there are a number of people I would like to thank. First and foremost, I want to pay tribute to all who hired me and provided a basis for writing this book: Rich Litt, who hired me for my first job out of college with no sales experience; Andy Sontag, who was much more than my first manager, a man who saw my potential, overlooked my weaknesses and put me in the right environment to thrive, and most importantly taught me how to wear a tie the correct way; to Joe Lupo, who truly cared about the art of selling and spent the time to teach me the fundamentals of the business environment; to Scott Taroff, who gave me my first opportunity to lead people; to Pat Kenney, who made a tough decision easy by giving me a great offer to come to my current firm.

I would like to thank all my friends, with whom I've competed against and have contributed to making me who I am today. What we did in the classrooms and fields we continue to do in the real world, pushing ourselves to reach that next level.

To my Mom and Dad, who spent their lives making sure their kids did not fail. Their sacrifice and unrelenting support could never be fully appreciated.

To my younger brother, who I look to as a role model. His value system as a man and support as a brother are unmatched.

To my coauthor, Scott O'Neil, who has never had a bad day in his life. A friend who is always great to be around, his positive influence and vision allowed this book to happen.

To my wife, and my two children Eric and Connor. They provide a motivation for me to give them all life has to offer.

SMO. A special thanks to people who have hired me along the way: Bruce Schilling for providing an internship, which cracked open the door to a field I love; Arnie Prives, who hired me in my first "real job" at the Nets as an assistant; Jon Spoelstra, for giving me my first promotion based on "potential"; Brett Yormark, for teaching me how to sell and being my coach in the office; Jeffrey Lurie, who is the best owner in the NFL; Joe Banner, who is a trusted friend and advisor, and Len Komoroski, who led through example and taught me the business; to David Stern, the greatest commissioner of all time in any sport, and the quintessential corporate leader, Russ Granik, a man who leads by example and always provides the voice of reason; Adam Silver, one of the most influential sports executive in the world; Bernie Mullin, who is one of the finest people and managers in the business; and Bill Sutton, who showed me "how to color out of the lines" and smile while doing it. Also, to Dr. Greg Bonner at Villanova, who gave me the opportunity to teach two semesters of Sports Marketing 101 at Villanova, an experience I will never forget.

To Eric Hinds, co-author, friend and confidante, one of the most competitive, intense, passionate people I have met and a person who truly understands and values friendship.

Equally as important, thanks to my friends who always root for me to win and continue to pick me up when I trip and fall. To the people I can call anytime for anything: Howie Nuchow, Chris Heck, Wilford Cardon, Adam Kanner, Seth Berger, Toby Shorter, Ryan Drew, and Peter Pilling.

To my Mom and Dad, because quite frankly, without them, there is no me. They provided everything I could ever need, being there when I needed them most and giving me every opportunity to succeed. Lastly, to my siblings and their spouses, Sean, Erin, Mike, Wendy, Matt, Stacy and Shannon, who keep me laughing through the insanity of it all and never let me forget the simple joy of life.

There are far too many people to list all those who have helped, continue to help and will help in the future ... if we forgot to mention your name, let us know (reason enough to write another book).

Table of Contents

Introduction   **10**

Chapter 1   Finding THE Job   **13**

Chapter 2   Thriving on Attitude   **36**

Chapter 3   Playing the Game   **54**

Chapter 4   Time Is on Your Side   **74**

Chapter 5   Scoring Goals   **89**

Chapter 6   Giving, Receiving and Enjoying Feedback   **101**

Chapter 7   Beaming with Confidence   **115**

Chapter 8   Managing Your Boss   **130**

Chapter 9   Constructing and Delivering the Message   **145**

Chapter 10   Change, Friend or Foe?   **159**

Chapter 11   Now What?   **171**

Introduction

Life is not easy when you are new to the rat race.

— *Scott M. O'Neil*

M*y free-spirited confidence and post-graduation summer vacation vanished with a single phone call on August 21, 1992. My father, a consultant, proudly called to say he had arranged an interview for me with a Fortune 500 company in Philadelphia. It was all over the second I hung up the phone. Freedom. Childhood. Fantasy Land. They all evaporated — and panic immediately set in. Reluctantly, I rearranged my beach time and basketball schedule, dusted off one of my two suits and headed back to Philadelphia for the interview.*

Unfortunately, my car broke down on the Garden State Parkway in New Jersey. I hitched a ride to Eric's apartment in Philadelphia to spend the night, not realizing until the next morning that my shirt, belt and shoes were locked in the trunk of my car at the service station. As I had so many times in school, I borrowed Eric's jeep and his roommate's oversized clothes.

Upon arrival, I jokingly explained my disheveled look and relayed the story of the car, belt and shoes to Paul Bugli, the Philadelphia area GM, who stared bewilderedly at me. Bugli lamented, "The people we want at this company are the people who will go out and buy a new belt and shoes and rent a car if there are any problems. We reward results here, not excuses. This job isn't for everyone and it isn't easy. We pay as well as anyone in the marketplace and recruiting is very competitive. I need to make sure you want this job and I am not convinced. You need to be ready. Are you ready? Why don't you take the weekend to think it over and get back to me first thing Monday morning." The meeting lasted ten minutes.

Embarrassment ... Anger ... Frustration ... Confusion ... Disappointment. Feelings of loneliness and failure wiped out any remnants of the confident, enthusiastic, free-spirited college graduate from the day before. I wasn't ready and Bugli knew it. Would I ever be ready? What would I tell my parents? Now what... ?

—Scott M. O'Neil

HOW-TO BOOK

Life is not easy when you are new to the "rat race." You will not know what to expect or what to do and you are playing a game without knowing the rules. Unfortunately, there are no Cliff Notes or tutors to help guide you through the confusing parts. To make matters worse, the stakes are higher and the pressure is on you. That is why we wrote this book. We have both had some terrific and gratifying experiences in the work world. Many errors are commonly committed by young professionals early in their careers. But we believe they can be avoided with some down-to-earth, practical guidance and a little effort.

This real-life, how-to book will help you through many of the difficult challenges you will encounter as you begin your professional life. The stories and experiences contained in this book are real. We combine our own experiences with those of other successful young business people to provide a best-practices, how-to guide to help you navigate through the rough waters of your early career.

XS AND OS

We have broken our findings out into 11 chapters, which represent 11 maxims of success for motivated and talented young professionals. In each chapter, you will find step-by-step frameworks to guide you from the initial job hunt to the interview to management reviews. The real-life stories are indented and italicized to draw additional attention. The stories are written in the first person in an attempt to capture the emotion of the moment. Our favorite quotes are periodically placed to try to accentuate a point or effectively set up a section or chapter.

Whenever possible, we used clear and concise step-by-step processes — and maxims to help you conceptualize, realize and put into practice promotion-worthy concepts. Take notes, make copies of the pages, rip them out of the book and tape them over your desk. The more you review these steps and take action, the more effective you will be at work.

Chapter 1

Finding
THE Job

Pleasure in the job puts perfection in the work.

— *Aristotle*

SCOTT M. O'NEIL AND ERIC J. HINDS

Everyone who wants to work will eventually find a job. The key to a successful and rewarding career is to find THE job. Finding THE job puts you in a position to experience a higher level of motivation, excitement and challenges. This chapter provides a practical and realistic step-by-step process to finding that job.

What are you going to do with the rest of your life? You are graduating in June. The question continues to pound you as your resume sits half completed on your PC. What is the hot industry? Do I need experience? Should you go into sales? Marketing? Accounting? Will anyone hire me?

Eric and Scott worked hard at finding a job. They traveled to bookstores, career-counseling sessions at school, visited the library, met with professors and professionals, talked to friends and sought counsel from relatives. Unfortunately, the harder they looked, the further they strayed from the course they'd originally set — finding a job that would provide stimulation, challenge, opportunity and fun. The search is filled with pressure from parents, friends and professors.

You need to get started now. Employers will not call you.

THROW YOUR HAT IN THE RING

A journey of a thousand miles must begin with the first step.
— Chinese Proverb

Before we can help you, you have to want to help yourself. Unfortunately a job will not fall in your lap; no one is going to call and seek you out for a position you would be perfect for, and you are not going to be recruited. This is the real world. Winning in the real world takes preparation, action and a willingness to seize the opportunities as they arise.

Preparation is essential. Are you ready? Is your resume complete? Do you have an interview suit? Is it dry cleaned and ready to go? Do you have your leather portfolio? Are you mentally ready to aggressively enter the arena?

Winners do what others are not willing and prepared to do.
— Anonymous

Succeeding in the rat race entails putting yourself in a job in which you will be comfortable. You are going to have to work hard, put in extra time and enjoy your work to be successful. Looking for a job is one of the most stressful times in life. Procrastination will magnify the stress. The only effective way to manage this stress is to throw your hat in the ring and get in the game.

ARE YOU A LOTTERY PICK?

It sounds funny to think that a job would come looking for you. But wouldn't it be nice if finding a job were as easy as sifting through the offers sent by would-be suitors in the mail, or fielding aggressive phone solicitations pleading with you to work for this firm or that organization? Unfortunately, if you are reading this book, you are probably not the Heisman Trophy winner (given to the nation's best college football player) anxiously awaiting draft day with a multi-million dollar signing bonus on the line. Like the rest of us, you are going to have to work to get hired at THE company with THE job. It is not going to come looking for you.

STEP 1: A MUST READ

It may seem ironic to have an author instructing you to go out and buy another book on a similar topic. However, this book is just too good to pass up: "What Color is Your Parachute?" by Richard Bowles. This book works because the author insists on asking and forcing the reader to answer questions important in finding a career and a future in a job. If you are confused about what you want to do, where you want to live and how you are going to get there — run, do not walk, to your nearest bookstore and pick up a copy of this book. It helped Scott sift through the many questions and concerns he had and directed him through a period of self doubt.

STEP 2: BE READY

A filly who wants to run will always find a rider.
                                                    — *Jacques Audiberti*

There is no light that goes on or buzzer that sounds to signal when you are ready, but you will definitely know if you are not ready. Scott was not ready when he visited the ADP general manager. Make sure you are ready to work when you begin your search; it will keep you hungry and pushing forward. It is not a requirement to spend the summer at the beach before you start work, but there will be no other time in your life that you have this opportunity. So take advantage of it.

Some people are ready to start the day school ends, others need a month or even a year. If you have the resources, freedom and money to travel across the country, take a trip to Europe, write a movie script, become a white-water rafting guide in Colorado or whatever else you have always wanted to do. Now is the time. Because once you get in the rat race it is very difficult to get out, even for a couple of weeks. Do what is right for you, but no matter what you decide to do, give it your all, buckle up and enjoy the ride.

STEP 3: COMMIT TO THE PROCESS

The average job search will take approximately three months. Prepare yourself. The only things you can control during this process is your work ethic and your attitude.

> **Work until it hurts.**
> — *Henry Royce, Rolls Royce*

GET OUT OF BED

Most recent college graduates have to recondition their internal clocks to get accustomed to waking up early in the morning. Start now! Also, many executives (successful ones anyway) are in the office early and are much more accessible. There are no gatekeepers (assistants) to block your access to reaching your potential employers on the phone. The early morning is also the best time to bypass the defense system put up around the executives and get into their voice mail.

> *I was just starting my network job search in graduate school and I was having difficulty getting to the top people in my field. I wanted to reach David Stern at the National Basketball Association and schedule a time to meet. He is very highly regarded throughout the industry as the top mind in the business. I was having trouble getting through until I called at 6:00 a.m., knowing that I would get an automated voice mailbox. The voice messaging system prompted the phone to access Commissioner David Stern's voicemail. I left a short, direct and aggressive message. The next day I received a call back and scheduled an interview.*
>
> — *Scott M. O'Neil*

CRAZY EIGHTS

Work at least an eight-hour day. This is the minimum number of hours you will be working when you get hired. Unless you have to work or have other commitments, make finding a job a priority. (See also, "Get out of Bed.")

NO MORE SIMPSONS

Turn off the television. Stop watching soap operas, "SportsCenter" for the third time, and re-runs of "Saved by the Bell." Television is your worst nightmare. Do NOT work on your resume, cover letters or anything else in front of the television. Do NOT make phone calls in front of the television. The job search is an important process (your career and happiness are at stake); make the right decisions. If you must watch television, do it over an allotted time for breakfast or lunch.

Spend time reading the newspaper and surfing the Web. Print out relevant articles that interest you about companies and industries you plan on attacking. Organize the information into relevant categories. Marketing, sales, etc. Save the information for cover letters, interviews and follow-up "thank-you notes." The information must be readily available and understandable whether you need it in three hours or three months. This information will help you be better prepared for interviews and provide an excellent resource for follow-up questions you may want to ask the interviewer.

Eliminate the Temptations

Procrastination is opportunity's assassin.

— *Victor Kiam*

Eliminate all procrastination tools at your fingertips. Limit Web surfing to research regarding your pending job search. Use the Internet as an asset, not as another distraction to keep you from completing your task. Take a sledgehammer to your Sony Playstation a.k.a anti-productivity station (or at least take it out of sight and disconnect it from the television).

Step 4: Identify Your Interests

People are more apt to enjoy their job if there is an inherent interest in the work. When you are interested and enjoy the work, you are more likely to work harder, smarter and more efficiently than if you had little or no interest in the work.

Do what you love, love what you do and deliver more than you promise.

— *Harvey Mackay*

Like most people in your situation, you probably have no idea what you want to do. That is okay and normal and not a barrier to finding THE job. One of the first steps to identifying THE job is to write down a list of your top 10 interests. The idea is to think out of the box. Ask friends, family, teachers, advisors, and anyone else for their input as you develop this list. This is a starting point to try to identify some target industries and companies to pursue.

Another useful tactic in developing your list is to surf the Internet. Use the interest as the keyword and surf from there. Consider this a do-not-surf-with-a-specific-agenda search; just let the information flow and use it to provide information about industries

Interest	Industries to Consider	Companies to Consider
Music	Music, Retail	BMG, Arista, MTV, Sam Goody Strawberries, Local Symphony
Clothes	Fashion, Design, Retail	Gap, Ralph Lauren, Kate Spade, Urban Outfitters, Nordstrom
Cars	Automobile, Suppliers, Dealers	GM, Ford, Chrysler, Car Dealership
Sports	Sports teams, Marketing Agencies, Events, Media	Professional Teams, Minor League Teams, Local Newspaper, Radio, CBS Sportsline, Colleges and Television Stations.
Stocks	Investment Banks, Mutual Fund Companies, Retail Banks, Commercial Banks, Insurance, Commodities Exchange	Merrill Lynch, Dean Witter, NYSE, NASDAQ, Chicago Commodities Exchange, Local Bank, Nationwide, State Farm, Goldman Sachs
Architecture	Contractors, Developers, Real Estate, Architecture	Morse Diesel, Turner Construction, Century 21, Local Architecture Firms
Art	Museums, Publishing, Printing	MOMA, Local Museum or Ballet, Local Printing Company, Hearst Publishing, Doubleday
Numbers	Accounting, Finance	Deloitte and Touche, Price Waterhouse/ Coopers, DLJ, Salomon Smith Barney, Morgan Stanley
Television	Television Production, Acting, Advertising	Fox, CNN, NBC, ABC, CBS, Nickelodeon, Lifetime, Foote Cone and Belding, Arnold Communications
High Tech	Computer Hardware, Software, Programming, E-Commerce Start-up	Dell, Gateway, Microsoft, Lotus, Amazon.com
Movies	Movie Studios, Retail, Production	Universal Studios, HBO, TMC, Disney, Blockbuster, Turner, Sony, AMC Theaters, General Cinema

Characteristic	Discipline to Consider
Outgoing	Sales
Leader	Management
Self-Starter	Entrepreneurial, Sales
Not Ambitious	Lifeguard
Interested in Process	Manufacturing, Engineering, Human Resources, R&D
Creative	Advertising, Marketing, Design
Likes Order	Manufacturing
Communication	Customer Service, Public Relations

and companies in the industries to consider. The intention of the example on the next page is to provide you a framework in constructing your own list.

This is just a guide for you to create your own list and get you started. Decide what your interests are and explore the possibilities.

If you still don't know after all this, ask yourself the following question: What would you do for a living if you did not have to work? (If the answer is head to the beach and hang with your friends, you are probably not ready.)

FURTHER TARGETING THE SEARCH

It is also important to better understand the role you would like to play in the organization. You probably will not be starting out as the president and CEO, so you will have to choose a discipline that allows your best fit in the organization. Again, ask friends, professionals, and professors where they see the best fit for you. Forget about your major in college. You are too young to be boxed into a specific discipline. When you begin your job, you will start with a clean slate.

Oftentimes it is beneficial to choose an area of the company that best fits your personality. The chart on page 20 is to help you align your personal characteristics with recommended disciplines to consider:

STEP 5: IDENTIFY THE TOP 20 COMPANIES WHERE YOU **WANT** TO WORK

**The very first step towards success in any occupation
is to become interested in it.**

— *Sir William Osler*

Identifying the top 20 places where you *want* to work is a step better than identifying the top 20 places you *think* you could get a job. Too many times job seekers simply settle for jobs displayed in the want ads or offered at the college job center. Others attack those jobs that are more easily accessible through family friends and contacts. The reality is that you will spend most of your waking hours working — shouldn't you choose where you spend that time? You have an opportunity to dictate where you will work. Take advantage of this opportunity.

To begin, first prioritize and rank what is important in your search.

      a. Is it a particular industry? High tech, sports marketing, health care, banking, consulting, etc.

      b. Is it a particular city? Philadelphia, New York, Los Angeles, Dallas, Boston, Washington, D.C., Portland, etc.

      c. Is it a particular discipline? Finance, sales, marketing, manufacturing, etc.

These questions need to be answered and prioritized. This process will help you self select your prospect during your search. For example, if you want to work in the financial services industry, geographically, you probably should target New York City, Chicago, San Francisco or Boston.

After prioritizing, list the top 20 places where you would most like to work. This will be a fluid list, in other words, constantly changing and adapting as you get additional information, leads and feedback.

**Success follows doing what you want to do.
There is no other way to be successful.**

— *Malcolm Forbes*

Once you have decided where you would like to live, as well as which industries you like to pursue, the next step is to identify the potential companies for your list. You must actively pursue the resources at your disposal to construct the list.

Trade Publications. Read any and all trade publications for the particular field you are looking to enter. If you are going into advertising, pick up "AdAge." If you are going into sales, buy "Selling." If you are entering the field of accounting, try "CFO." Most local chambers of commerce sell the "Book of Lists" for most major cities in the United States, which is an excellent starting point.

Internet. Use the industry as the key word in the search engine sites.

Professors. Speak to the professors at your school teaching in the particular fields that you have chosen to pursue. These professors will be able to provide direction and guidance.

Career Center. This is where the career center can be an excellent research vehicle for you.

Talk to Friends. People love to talk about themselves and will share their experiences if you are willing to ask. Talk to friends, family, and everyone else you know and let them know you are looking. Ask for advice, recommendations and help.

> *I was two years out of college living in California, pretty exciting, being a Jersey boy. My first employment was a sales assistant with Knoll Furniture selling modular office systems. The starting salary was $25,000 a year plus bonus, again not a bad set-up for just being out college — single, living in LA, working for a great company, meeting all kinds of people and making money. Life was good, but I found myself going to Dodger, Lakers and Kings games and every time thinking, I want to pursue my college degree (sports marketing) and get with a professional sports team. So I came to a tough decision to move back East and go after the job of my true desire, pro sports. I can remember my co-workers at the time wishing me luck and saying how "cool" that would be to get that kind of job.*
>
> *Sure it would be cool, but the reality was that landing my dream job would take a lot of work. The very first thing I did was to sit down and call every professional team in the New York metropolitan area and ask for their director of marketing and mailing address. Second was to send my limited resume to every pro sports team (Knicks, Rangers, Devils, Nets, Mets, Yankees, Islanders). I was fired up! As I followed up with phone calls and started to receive those standard letters with the words "Thanks, We'll keep*

your resume on file," discouragement started to hit.

I knew I needed to break through to make an impact. Finally, I was able to catch the marketing director for the New Jersey Nets on the phone and actually have a real conversation. He told me that they might be looking for a salesperson and to speak to the VP of sales. My foot was in the door and I wasn't going to pull it out! I set up the meeting, met with the entire sales group at the team. My message was simple to management. "I will bust my tail and out-sell every person on the staff, just give me the chance."

I guess my sincerity showed through. I got the job, became a top salesperson and even got asked to speak at one of the sports marketing classes at Guilford College on a visit to my old school. Although I've moved on now I will always treasure and remember that early feeling of success. Know exactly what type of job you want, set your sights, go after with true persistence and don't look back!"

—Dan Hauck, Quadrant HealthCom Inc.

STEP 6: IDENTIFY AND CONTACT YOUR NETWORK

The smartest thing I ever said was, "Help me!"
—Anonymous

This is a very uncomfortable step for most people graduating college, yet probably the most important step in finding THE job. If there is one thing to take away from this book, let it be recognizing the importance of developing your network. Wake up and smell the coffee. Remember the old saying: It is not what you know, it is who you know. Nothing could be closer to the truth. If you have not started already, keep a database of people you meet.

Skill is fine, and genius is splendid, but the
right contacts are more valuable than either.
— Sir Archibald McIndoe

Have you ever heard of six degrees of separation? In most industries it probably is closer to two degrees. After identifying interests and listing your top 20 places you would like to work, the next step is to identify and contact your network:

- **Buy ACT! Or a Rolodex.** If you do not currently have a current database or Rolodex, you need to purchase one.

- **Make an All-Inclusive List.** List 100 people you know. List family members, in-laws, friends, friends' parents, high school teachers, professors, coaches, neighbors, old bosses, etc.

- **Reach Out and Touch Someone.** Give them a call and tell them about your active search.

- **Ask for Help.** Let them know you need some assistance.

- **Informational Interviews.** Set up a time to meet if it is convenient. The more people you see, the more exposure you will have to different viewpoints and the better off you are.

- **Ask for Referrals.** Make sure to ask if there is anyone else you could be put in touch with who might be helpful in your search.

The old saying, "It's not what you know, it's who you know" is only half right. It should be said, "It's not who you know, it's who THEY know." During my junior year in college an interested cousin of mine set up a series of meaningful informational interviews. You know the kind, where the person sitting across from you doesn't have a job to offer, but if you're lucky you can learn a bit about them and how they broke into the biz.

I was hot for a career in advertising and I was meeting a creative master from Earle Palmer Brown in Philadelphia. His reputation and the hot streak his agency was riding were enough to get me focused on this interview. The meeting went well. It ended with the obligatory, "Stay in touch" only this time I had every intention of doing just that. Once a month for the next 16 months, I called or wrote Ed Tettemer at Earle Palmer Brown. He and his agency were riding high, winning business and awards. When I graduated I was hoping to join his shop. It didn't happen, but I kept in touch. Several times a year for the next two years I would drop him a note, give a call, keep tabs on the agency and congratulate his wins. I also let him know what I was up to and what I was learning in an unrelated field. He knew I wanted advertising and he knew I wanted his shop.

One day, out of the blue, he called with an opening in the account services department. I jumped at the chance. I got the job and worked for Earle Palmer Brown for the next three years. To this day I speak with Ed several times a year. He and I have crossed paths again and again over the past 15 years. We have sent each other leads and new clients, found new talent for each other's companies and become good friends. The next time someone says, "Stay in touch," take them up on it.

—Jeffrey Smith, freelance producer

Keep the end in mind. Continue to get closer to the top 20 companies you have on your list. You will be pleasantly surprised how quickly you can get in to see someone if you put your mind to it. Networking is the key to placing you in a job where you can be successful.

I was confused and frustrated coming out of Villanova. There were two things on my mind: One, I was in debt and needed money. Two, I did not have a job lined up and had very few prospects. It did not take a rocket scientist to realize that this combination would not fare well with my parents, who had spent the last four years working Saturdays, passing on vacation and struggling to help pay for my education. To top it all off, I was beginning to get frustrated with the whole process. I just needed a chance.

I knew I would be successful in sales and thought the pace would fit my lifestyle. I just was not sure of what I should sell and how to go about getting a job in sales. After three months of fruitless interviews and unproductive dealings with headhunters, I called my friend's dad, Dr. O'Neil. Doc listened very carefully to my situation, asked where I wanted to live and said he would call back in 10 minutes. Doc called back with a scheduled interview for me in a company for which he consulted called ADP (Automatic Data Processing).

Dr. O'Neil recognized that I needed training, structure, and a little room for growth. After three interviews, ADP offered me a job, which I accepted.

— Eric J. Hinds

Eric later learned that the interviewers were both very skeptical, but hired Eric on the basis of Dr. O'Neil's recommendation. It was clear that Eric was given the opportunity because of a relationship he had formed with a family friend.

Step 7: Do Your Homework

Before everything else, getting ready is the secret of success.

— *Henry Ford*

Whether you are meeting with your uncle, brother in-law, neighbor or friend's father, it is important to be prepared for the meeting. Before interviewing, do your homework. The Internet makes life a lot easier in this regard. Punch in the company name as a key word after summoning one of the search engines. Read the 10 most recent articles on the company. If the company is public, go to www.pcquote.com or one of the myriad other Web sites providing information on public companies. You can never know too much about a company you are interviewing for. Who are its customers? What product or service does it offer? What do the prospective markets look like? Who are its suppliers? What is the senior management team's background? How does it measure success?

Another productive way to locate information about a company is to speak with someone who previously or currently works there. The closer the person is to the job you are interviewing for, the more likely the information will be of help. There may be certain "hot buttons" a company or certain individual looks for in a prospective candidate. Information is power and it will help you prepare intelligent and well-thought out questions to ask toward the close of the interview.

Research and company knowledge demonstrates an overall interest and commitment to excellence. This will differentiate you as a candidate in an interview and tip the scales in your favor.

Step 8: Understanding Where You Add Value

Know thyself.

— *Suzanne DePasse*

After you have done your homework, you need to understand where you can add value to a company. It is important to have a clear understanding and be able to articulate where and how you feel you can contribute.

Being true to yourself is essential throughout your career. You must be able to understand your strengths and identify opportunities. Look for opportunities that offer you the chance to leverage your strengths. A new boss was hired to oversee the marketing of the

New Jersey Nets. The new boss, Jon Spoelstra, called Scott into his office for an interview to learn more about what Scott did and to discuss his future with the organization. Scott knew that his strengths would be best accentuated in a sales role.

> Boss: What do you do?
>
> Scott: I am an assistant. I do a lot of support work. Actually, anything anyone asks of me. I put on the Chuck Daly Welcome Party, Sponsor Kids' Day, run the Executive Club. I do a lot of things.
>
> Boss: What do you want to do?
>
> Scott: I want to sell sponsorships.

Scott recognized his strength and sensed an opportunity. He was promoted a week later and became the youngest sponsorship salesperson in the NBA at just 22 years old.

First jobs are usually entry-level positions that require various elements to ensure success. A big challenge is trying to understand where you can add value to a company and thus convey that to the interviewer. Unfortunately, there are usually few transferable skills you bring from college that will help you in the work world.

Keeping that in mind, it is important to stay focused on what you can add and the message you can convey. You will add value because you will be reliable, work hard, arrive at work before your boss, have passion about the job and a willingness to start immediately. List 10 messages you will convey in your interview. Get comfortable with the phrases and make them part of yourself.

For example: Message 1: "I am the type of person who enjoys work. I will be the first person in the office in the morning and the last person to leave at night."

FIND A COMPETITIVE ADVANTAGE

The key is finding the competitive advantage. Look out of the box and expand your search. Remember that you are graduating with 5,000 students at a university or college. They all have many of the same experiences you have (not to mention degree). Therefore, it is often beneficial to embark on a network job search outside of the campus career center. The goal is to get in a position in which you can differentiate yourself.

STEP 9: WHAT IS THE INTERVIEWER LOOKING FOR?

Scott and Eric have had multiple opportunities to interview for jobs as well as interview others for positions in their respective companies. Therefore, there is a clear understanding of the traits that an interviewer is looking for when filling an entry-level position.

Interviewers are often asking themselves the following questions as they are interviewing for entry-level positions:

- Will you work hard? (Unless you are looking for a government job — hard workers are always welcome and usually in short supply).

- Will you represent the company well?

- Will you embarrass the interviewer by not delivering on the job?

- Do you have good references?

- Are you a team player?

- Do you have good communication skills?

- Will you add to the organization, group and division?

- Will you deliver? (More than pizza.)

TIPS FOR STANDING OUT OF CROWD

**Do not follow where the path may lead,
go instead where there is no path and leave a trail.**
— *Anonymous*

Often times there will be hundreds of applicants seeking the position for which you are interviewing. It is important to take deliberate steps to stand out in the crowd. The following is a list to help you along the way:

- Answer specific questions.

- Offer examples to help clarify your points.

- Get solid references. Have your references proactively call the interviewer. Spend extra time to coach the references on the importance of the job and make sure they are well versed about the person they are calling, what the job requirements are and why you will be a good fit for the position.

- Look like you are maximizing your time. Bring reading materials to the reception area. Be aware and alert. Little things matter. Bring a pen and paper.

- Introduce yourself to receptionists and remember their names.

- Give a firm handshake and look people in the eye when you talk to them.

- Always close the interview by asking the question, "What is the next step?"

I graduated from college and took a job for the money. Learned a little bit but wasn't passionate about it. Quit and coached part-time high school basketball while making a list of my dream jobs. Working for the 76ers was #1. Networked and found a family friend at the company. He gave me the name of a manager who was hiring. I showed up on their door step one Monday morning with no appointment. When he arrived, he claimed he was in meetings all morning. I told him I would wait until the afternoon. When he finally saw me, he did everything he could to get me out of his office. I convinced him to 'play' interview with me so I could at least learn.

After a couple minutes of the 'play' interview he told me he had to go to another meeting and couldn't hire me anyway. I asked him why. He told me it was because he was looking for a ticket salesperson. This person would need intimate knowledge of the arena (Spectrum). I then asked him if he had a map of the arena handy and that I would have the arena sections memorized in 10 minutes. That got me a formal interview later that week, which ultimately led to a job offer. The moral I took from this was to: 1) decide what you want (career); 2) use your networking skills to get in the door; and 3) use your passion and persistence to get the job.

—Ron Skotarczak, And 1

STEP 10: BE CREATIVE IN YOUR FOLLOW-UP

Everyone sends a thank-you letter after an interview. Canned thank-you letters are the norm and will not get you any closer to the job. The key is to differentiate yourself with a thank-you letter.

The standard follow-up. The content should be relevant to the conversation you had in the interview. Bring up something specific you discussed in the interview, which will let the interviewer know you actively listened and spent extra time writing your thank-you.

Thinking out of the box. Do you really want the job? How badly? Companies are looking for people who think creatively. The following are examples of people who went above and beyond in the follow-up and got hired!

There is no traffic jam on the extra mile.

— *Anonymous*

I had some friends already working at ADP and it seemed like a great work environment. After interviewing with ADP, one of my friends had said my chances were about 50/50 of getting the job. I knew I had to do something to convey to them that I really wanted the job and would go the extra mile. I went to Kinkos and enlarged a check which read, "Pay to the order of ADP for $100,000" and signed my name. I had it FedExed to the interviewer the next day. I attached a note, which read: "These are the types of commission checks we will be seeing when you hire me." I really think this put me over the top and got me the job.

— *Tom Logio, Superior Group and Glacier Systems*

Deutsch, Inc. was the hottest advertising agency in New York City and that was where I wanted to be. They had just won the Tanqueray gin account and were looking for an account executive to put the brand on the map. It seemed as if everyone I knew in the business wanted this job. I scored an interview, which went very well, but I knew that would not be enough. I sent a bottle of Tanqueray to the advertising agency president, who had recently interviewed me. I changed the label to read Mike O'Neil and Tanqueray — The Perfect Match. The note attached to the bottle read: We could celebrate my hiring over drinks! I got the job and the 25% pay raise that went with it.

— *Michael O'Neil, Get Well Network*

I interned at the New Jersey Nets for an entire summer and did not seem to be getting any closer to landing a job. Graduation was approaching and I was starting to sweat it. I knew the VP of sales had an ego the size of Mt.

Rushmore and loved creativity and persistence. I decided to go the creative route and it worked. I sent mini-basketballs to him on consecutive days. The notes on the balls read: *With the 1st Pick in the 1992 Draft ... The New Jersey Nets ... Select ... Howard Nuchow!*

— Howard Nuchow, Mandalay Sports and Entertainment

I interviewed with a manufacturing company that was struggling. Both people I interviewed with stressed the need for go-getters. It appeared as if they were looking for someone who would really hustle and get after it. I knew this is where I could stand out and make an impression. I rushed to the mall to pick up a thank-you card and hand-delivered the note later the same afternoon. On top of the thank-you note was a Post-It© note that read, "Some things just cannot wait for the U.S. mail." I was offered a job that afternoon.

— Pat Toland, Huber Enterprises

I had interned with three different sports marketing companies and felt I was ready for the real world. All I needed was a chance. I had an interview with the NBA League office. I had always wanted to work there and my chance was within reach. I decided to send an autographed basketball to the interviewer with a note attached reading: "The first assist of many." I was called in for a second interview two days later and ended up getting the job.

— Lisa Reynolds, TOBI Productions

You must differentiate yourself. Be creative. As corny as it may seem, companies are looking for out-of-the-box risk-takers willing to go the extra mile. Finding a job is not an easy process. It takes hard work, commitment and proper planning. You will be rewarded for your effort. Almost everyone has a job. The key is to focus on THE job.

STEP 11: WHEN ALL ELSE FAILS

If one or more of the companies you are targeting is not hiring, consider a post-degree internship. Internships are an excellent way to gain experience and contacts in a company or field you are interested in working in. More importantly, internships provide a first-hand look and feel for whether an industry suits you, while offering a great way to test the experience and improve your resume. There is also the opportunity to explore different disciplines in the company, and network with people in entry level jobs to see if they are doing the kind of work you would be interested in. They often lead to full-time employment, if you do a good job.

I had just graduated from law school and was waiting for an offer from a non-profit organization I'd worked for a few years earlier. Because the organization was undergoing a major restructuring, I knew it would be at least a few months before I heard anything from them. So, just in case, I started looking for a back-up position.

My wife's business partner knew of an entertainment attorney, Louise, who happened to be looking for an entry level attorney. I sent in my resume, called to set up an interview and, shortly thereafter, was sitting in front of Louise having a great interview. She and I talked for almost an hour (she still says it was the "best" interview she ever had with a potential employee — certainly not the first time I've heard that). Near the end of the interview, however, a wrench was thrown into my well-oiled plan: Louise looked at my resume again and realized that I had in fact GRADUATED from law school. It ends up that Louise had just hired a new associate, was now looking for a secretary (or "administrative assistant" for those of you into semantics), and thought that that was the position for which I was interviewing.

Upon digesting this unexpected depreciation in my already less-than-stellar fortunes, I asked Louise what the job would entail. She explained that it would involve answering phones, typing contracts, filing — standard fare. I quickly weighed my options and decided this remained an opportunity worth pursuing. I told Louise that although I was shortly expecting an offer from my former company (honesty still being the best policy!), I'd be happy to cover for her while she continued to look for a permanent secretary. I explained that I was an excellent typist (two classes in high school — don't laugh, TWO easy "As" AND that's where all the pretty girls were!) and didn't mind answering phones (it's not like I went to Harvard and was above that sort of thing). I also felt the position would allow me to learn a little bit about entertainment and simultaneously make a few connections that might prove useful in the nonprofit sector. Louise agreed to hire me and, to make a long story short (no, it's not too late), within a month she'd made me a legal associate.

I didn't leave for almost five years! Ten years later, I'm still in the entertainment industry, running a music production company and eternally grateful to Louise for giving me what most law school grads would consider a lesser opportunity. I'm also glad that I did not allow a big head (i.e., ego) to keep me from slipping through that brief crack in the door to entertainment.

— Toby Shorter, A Touch of Jazz

Intern ... With a Degree?

Nobody graduating from college wants to hear about participating in an internship. After all, most internships are unpaid or at least underpaid. We all envision ourselves in a high powered, high paying position. Let's wake up to reality — that is not how a business career begins. It is all part of the process of working your way up the corporate ladder. There is no better low-risk way to find out if a company, industry, department and discipline area is a fit for you. Internships are also a great way to "get your foot in the door" in industries that are difficult to break in to.

When students graduate from college there is tremendous pressure internally, from friends, family and society, to get a job right away. The reality is that the best time to start is when you are ready. The best place to work is not always the first offer that comes your way. Landing THE job only happens if you decide to take a proactive and controlled approach.

On May 10, 1992, I graduated from Villanova University, ready to take on the "real world." I had the good fortune to secure an internship with the Baltimore Orioles class AA team in Hagerstown, Md. I had saved up about $2,000, which I was to live on for the summer as I was determined to make my internship turn into a full time job by Labor Day. This was the beginning, so I thought, to become a star in the sports marketing industry.

I never told my parents or friends that I would not have benefits or a salary for that matter; reality was that I would be making $15 per game with no guarantee of full-time employment. Failure was not an option. I would get a full-time job and I would make it in sports; there was no plan B. The team set me up with housing for $170 per month sharing a basement with two Dominican ball players who spoke little English. May 11, 1992, first day of work, the GM of the ball club called me at about 8:30 a.m. and gave me a tour of the depressed ball park in my new sad city of Hagerstown, which is about 10 miles from the West Virginia border. After a 15-minute tour, we stood in the dugout and he asked me what I thought. Confidently I replied, "This looks great but I can't believe the grounds crew has allowed grass to grow in several spots of the infield dirt on an AA field."

He said nothing and brought me to the bullpen where he picked up an empty bucket. "Here is your first assignment. Go take all of the grass out of the infield dirt." Over the next three hours, I found myself picking and pulling every blade of grass and every weed while ruining my newly pressed dress pants and polo shirt. *Lesson #1: Never bitch about something that you won't or can't fix yourself.* Later on that week the Hagerstown Suns were scheduled for a home stance and this was my first chance to make an impact and impress. What would they have me work on? Would it be handling the media and players or assisting the coaches and scouts or working the press box? I found myself wearing an apron, taking grief from 9- and 10-year-olds working the slightly less-than-glamorous "speed pitch game." All that I could think was, "What the hell did I get myself into? Don't they know that I have degree from a fine institution? I was a big shot a week ago." *Lesson #2: I was starting over; no job was too small.* In order to gain respect I needed to be the best at the smallest of the small jobs before I got a chance at the bigger jobs.

The summer continued, pride was out the window and I needed a plan. The owner and his wife would frequent games and after a few introductions and cold responses from the less-than-outgoing team owner, I recognized how I would win that full-time job. It would be through the wife, which would take me directly to the owner himself. I sold lemonade instead of beer (she liked lemonade). I worked the open grill (she liked hamburgers, not hot dogs). I sold programs on the third base side of the stadium (she always sat in the front row on the shaded side). At every encounter, I gave her a wide smile and a kind word. I became tight with the stadium game day workers and they would eventually call me on the radio when the owner and his wife entered through the front gate. For me, this is when game time really started. I ran through the stands selling lemonade like no other vendor, yelled the loudest while selling programs and threw out all inhibitions with any other of my game day duties. This was not to "fool" anyone; my agenda was always clear: I would do anything and everything to get a full-time job. *Lesson #3: Throw away your pride, have a great attitude, always hustle and always smile.*

Late August, time was running out, I was searching and asking for answers *and not getting any. I finally was able to have a sit-down meeting with the owner and he told me that the team would be moving at the end of the season. He said that he liked my hustle and charisma, which I am certain came directly from his wife. He would see what he could do but would not have any answers until after the season. The last game was on Labor Day and still no word. I came to work the next day not knowing my future. One by one, each full-time employee met with the owners and their brass. One by one, each and every full-time employee came out of the office with their employment terminated. I was the last to enter; they offered me a full-time job with the Class A Frederick Keys as ticket manager and sponsorship sales executive. Lesson #4: Establish a plan and stick with it. Sometimes you get lucky.*

— Chris Heck, Villanova Sports Marketing

Sailing the Internships

Internships often provide you information on what you might want to do as well as what you do not want to do. The important thing is to gain experience.

I wanted to go into big business. Fortune 500 or bust, I thought. So I accepted an internship with First Brands Corp. in Connecticut. First Brands produces name brands such as STP, Prestone @, Simonize and Glad @ products. I worked in a lab testing the strength and consistency of plastic containers. The pay was great, but I dreaded going back to work each Monday. It seemed like I did not move from the work bench the entire summer. I quickly learned that being in a lab, testing products did not suit my needs. It was also a very corporate and somewhat stuffy environment, which was not ideal for my personality either.

— Scott O'Neil

It is great when you find yourself in an internship that you love. The work is exciting and the environment is a place where you could see yourself thriving.

I interned in the marketing department for Advantage International in Washington, D.C., which at the time was the third largest sports marketing firm in the world. This experience exposed me to a world of business where people enjoyed coming to work. Advantage was a high energy company packed with young professionals who worked hard and played hard. Despite the pay of

Chapter 2

Thriving on Attitude

The only thing you can control is your attitude.

— Anonymous

$0 for a summer of hard work, the experience was invaluable in helping to introduce me to the industry I knew I would eventually join, build my resume and make lifelong contacts. But most importantly, I discovered that the successful people all came in early and stayed late, dressed in a similar way, conducted themselves professionally, etc. These experiences would provide the road map for how I conducted himself in my first job with the New Jersey Nets.

— Scott M. O'Neil

Other internships provide a roadmap for the future, setting the table for what needs to be done to get to where you want to be.

Following graduation, I interned for a summer at a large brokerage house. The experience was eye opening and rewarding. I learned that I was ready and would be most successful in a high-pressure sales environment. I learned

Action	Why I Can Control	Why I Lose Control
Arriving Early at Work	Get to bed early, wake up early, be prepared	Traffic, weather, power outage
Bad Weather	Proper clothes, stay indoors	Weatherman is wrong, storm is surprise
High Sales	Make calls, deliver top notch pitch, good appointments, solid follow-through	Bad economy, service out of touch, market saturated
Good Lunch	Pick favorite place, order reliable meal	New waitress, chef quit, new management
Way Boss Speaks to You	Overdeliver, first to office, exceed expectations	Kid cut from soccer team, boss's boss unhappy, stocks are down
Good Attitude	YOUR CHOICE	NO REASON

how to dress and act professionally in a corporate setting. I worked additional hours and developed a great relationship with my boss. But, I also knew that I was not prepared or confident enough to ask people to hand over their money for me to manage. I knew I had to get my feet wet somewhere else.

— Eric J. Hinds

Five years later, Eric's boss from his internship hired him away from ADP for five times more than they would have paid if he had worked there right out of college.

Be willing to chop vegetables to learn from the best chef in the world. Jobs early in your career are stepping stones to bigger and better jobs down the road. You are going to have to sacrifice, plan, prepare, act, react and deliver. It is all at your fingertips. The road is not easy, but it will be rewarding and worth the trip when you land THE job.

Okay, you have successfully identified and obtained THE Job. The next great challenge on the road to success is maintaining the proper positive attitude. This chapter is designed to help you realize the importance of having and conveying this attitude to others.

There is no way to prepare for uncertainties or predict the future. Life is like an elevator, full of ups and downs. It is essential to focus your energy on what you can control: your attitude. Focusing on a positive attitude will attract positive people and help you navigate through difficult situations at work and in life.

DRIVING IN CONTROL

Put this book down for a few minutes, get a pad and pen and list the things you have control over. As you will see from the following chart, the only thing you have full control over is your attitude and how you react to situations. Review a common workday:

**Things turn out best for people who
make the best of the way things turn out.**

— *Anonymous*

Five percent of your lot in life is dictated by what happens to you. The other 95% is controlled by your reaction to the initial 5%. It all revolves around your attitude. The magic is that your attitude is 100% under your control. The way you look at your work and life will differentiate you from your peers.

Things are not always going to be perfect at work. There is more likelihood of problems than perfection. Problems occur regularly: People quit, customers complain, the weather is not always warm and sunny, but you cannot control those happenings. You control your attitude and how you react to all the uncertainties and surprises presented day to day.

The ultimate measure of a man is not where he stands in moments of convenience, but where he stands at times of challenge and controversy.
— *Martin Luther King Jr.*

I always think of the Bruce Springsteen quote, "I can't tell my courage from my desperation," so I don't know if my bold, aggressive salesmanship was from courage or desperation of nearly going belly up and getting forced to be a loan officer at some crappy bank.

I called a client who I thought may have a $10 million mobile home park mortgage deal. He said, "Too late, I am signing a deal today." I said, "That would be a huge mistake. I will be in your office in one hour. Have your income statements ready."

I closed the deal for $10,500,000 and made a $61,000 commission. I saved the borrower $80,000 per year in interest. Another mhp guy heard I was doing the deal and prior to closing he said, "If you deliver the $10.5 mil for my friend you will have my next package of deals." Later that year I closed $20,000,000 in parks with the second borrower. Since that time, 1997, I have been involved in more than $300,000,000 in mhp park deals in 20 states, fees probably in excess of $3,000,000. I don't know if it was courage or desperation that made me so aggressive, But it worked, thank God.

— Gerry DiMarco, Security Mortgage Group

This task is not always easy. Everyone gets upset, angry and frustrated. We all have certain buttons or cues that set us off, but maintaining a positive disposition at work is essential to your success. Look for the positive, the silver lining in every dark cloud. The reality is usually not as bad as it often appears and by staying positive and reacting in the right way the problems can be mitigated. No work-related problem is ever worth changing your attitude. Problems, disasters and change all bring opportunity for creative solutions and positive leadership. Controlling how you act at all times is crucial to building your future. No one will remember you when the times are good because at that moment everyone has a good attitude. You are remembered positively for the tough times when you remained focused on your positive attitude. That attitude will always get you over the top.

Nothing great in the world has been accomplished without passion.
— George Hegel

Attitude and passion go hand in hand in determining your lot in life. Passion is the true essence and determinant of success. Passion is the inner drive that can bring out the best or worst for a person in any situation. It is a catalyst that can drive our mind and soul to accomplish anything we choose. Unfortunately, most people have difficulty being passionate about work. What are you passionate about? Is it your college football team, exercising, cooking, family or religion? Identify your passions in life and look to bridge some of that energy to your work life.

Fans will paint their faces, buy the new team jersey and tailgate at 8:00 a.m. for a 4:00 p.m. game in sub-zero temperature. Those same people forget to polish their shoes, show up at 8:00 a.m. for work and fail to bring that same energy, enthusiasm and desire to their jobs. The task will be easier if you have followed our advice in Chapter 1 and found THE job. Working in THE job will not make you passionate, but it will provide you the best opportunity to bring passion into your work. You need to find a way to transform the energy, enthusiasm and overall passion you find in other aspects of your life into your job.

A year after starting my job at Pacific Gas and Electric Company (of Erin Brockovich/Julia Roberts notoriety), I had the opportunity to have lunch with the woman who interviewed me on campus and eventually championed me for the job. Over some incredibly fresh seafood dishes, we got honest on why exactly she made sure I was brought on board. She answered, "Well, most people we see at the entry level are competent, especially coming out of Berkeley. We see impressive grades, over-busy extracurricular schedules, some great characters, but over the years I have found one trait that stands out as being rewarding from an employer standpoint: enthusiasm. I'll take a middling academic performer with high energy over a straight A student who comes across as needing a cattle prod just to walk down the hall. Later on in a career, leadership aptitude is important, but early on it's energy level. I hired you because you were clearly more enthusiastic and, by extension, more optimistic than everyone else we interviewed. And it has showed in your work here. I give you the tough, high profile assignments, sometimes over more senior people, because I know you will throw all your energy into it and can literally will something to get done based on your enthusiasm alone. Your energy has been your greatest asset, that and your ability to order great white wine with lunch."

— Meriko Sarmiento Deutsche Banc Alec, Brown Inc.

A JOB OFFER

Maintaining a positive attitude is not always easy, especially with entry-level jobs. By some combination of luck, fate and circumstance, Scott received and accepted an offer as marketing assistant to the senior vice president of sales and marketing for the New Jersey Nets basketball team of the NBA. At a whopping salary of $15,000 per year, in the most expensive area to live in the country, who would mind zero vacation days, typing memos, getting morning coffee and picking up the boss's dry cleaning? (Sarcasm, off.)

Looking back, the job seemed like slave labor or at least a recipe for disaster. However, the job paid almost two times as much as his bouncing job at the Princeton Bar and Grill at the Jersey shore. More importantly, it was THE job in the industry Scott loved. It was a foot in the door and Scott was ready to take advantage of it. Scott's parents smiled for the first time in three months, finally able to visualize a return on their $100,000 investment.

After struggling through three months of intensive networking, sending out resumes and cold calling, the job offer was a huge lift. The feelings of frustration and self-doubt he had felt throughout the job process would push him each day to work hard and truly appreciate this opportunity.

WORK HOURS

Each organization has its own culture, which dictates when people arrive in the morning and when people leave in the evening. As a general rule, come to work 30 minutes earlier than your boss and leave 30 minutes after the boss leaves at night. Make the early morning entry a habit. Be the first person in each day to turn off the alarm or bring in the paper or say hello to the night watchman. Word will get around very quickly.

> *The first day on the job had finally arrived. I was so anxious and excited about my first day at the New Jersey Nets, I showed up at 7:00 a.m. There was no one in sight. The doors were locked and the lights were off. I drove around the arterial surrounding Meadowlands Arena. After circling the 'track' about 25 times, I approached the office door (which was locked) and found a seat in the foyer. I waited about an hour until the receptionist pulled in and unlocked the door at 8:45 a.m. The receptionist had no idea who I was or what I was doing there — what a start!*

> *— Scott M. O'Neil*

Coming in early would become a regular happening for Scott, especially after he was given a key to the office door. Despite what you may think, people do notice. What will differentiate you from your peers in an entry-level job is your attitude and work ethic. Putting time in at the office will send a clear message to others that you are dedicated, serious and committed to making your stay at this organization a success. This is not to suggest that coming in early to read the paper, gossip and surf the Web are sure paths to the executive suite. Work at work. Coming in early will set the tone positively as to how you are perceived. Make coming in early a habit.

> *I was working on a project and managing five staff people. One of my young staffers approached me and asked why I got in at 7:00 a.m. each morning (an hour and one-half before everyone else). That is the only time I can get any "work" done, I thought to myself. I carefully chose my words and then explained: I have deliverables due each day and need the additional time to focus on those projects. Nine to 5 is spent making sure that you and the staff stay as productive and successful as possible. When you are not on track or slip and fall, I don't stand a chance. That additional time keeps me organized, focused and ahead of the workload.*

> *— Jeffrey Piluso, AT Kearny*

Don't Get Too Comfortable

The greatest discovery of my generation is that man can alter his life by simply altering his attitude of mind.
— William James

It is important to stay focused and on the right path toward success. Stay with the program that brought you success.

> I worked with a young, hot-shot at ADP-Princeton, N.J. Brian was on the fast track and could sell more effectively than anyone else could in the office. Brian came in early, stayed late and even came in on Saturdays to finish paperwork so he could concentrate on sales during the week. Brian blew his peers away and began to receive a lot of positive feedback. However, about six months into the job, Brian learned he did not need to work as hard as he currently had been. Brian started to slide into work around 9:00 a.m. and was out the door around 5:00 p.m. and found he still managed to remain in the middle of the pack. Because of his strong start, he ended the year 110% of plan.
>
> As always, bad habits catch up with you — and for Brian that meant that midway through his second year he began to bomb out. Brian's manager started to turn up the heat. Brian did not enjoy the extra attention he was receiving and contemplated leaving the company. I spoke with Brian one morning about the importance of getting back to the basics. Brian's personality had gotten him through some tough spots before, but it would take good old-fashioned work ethic this time. The next week Brian changed his work methods and his attitude. The first change he made was getting to work at 7:00 each morning and properly preparing for the day. Brian achieved President's Club that year and although he left ADP, he continues to get up early and attributes this to his continued success. He is still the first person in the office and looks forward to the President's Club trips each year.
>
> — Eric J. Hinds

Attitude is Positively Important

Why is it that some sports franchises always seem to win and others seem destined to lose year after year? Often times it is a winning attitude that players, coaches, owners and front office personnel become accustomed to. Winning is a way of life. It is a decision and commitment people make. Conversely, some franchises cannot do anything right. No matter how many good players, draft picks and quality coaches come in, they cannot seem to win. Television commentators often talk about these franchises and young players needing to learn how to win. These commentators are only partially correct. It all starts with the attitude, from top to bottom. Why do the

Chicago Cubs and the Los Angeles Clippers consistently hover around the cellar? It all starts with attitude.

When fate hands you a lemon, make lemonade.
— Dale Carnegie

When we started an NHL expansion team in Nashville, we didn't have a logo or team name. About two months before we started our first season, we also didn't have a ticket operations person because he "couldn't handle the stress and number of work hours." He quit at 1:15 p.m., and walked out the door at 1:16 p.m.

With our first season looming, and the deadline to reserve, print and deliver season ticket holders additional single game tickets the next day, I had to jump into action. As the VP of ticket sales, I started fulfilling the orders myself even though I had limited knowledge of the process. I had no choice if we were going to meet the deadlines we put forth to our season ticket holders. I started at 3 p.m. and did not stop until I apparently fell asleep in my chair sometime between 5 and 6 a.m. Other staff started to come into the office and one of my staff members actually knocked over my chair to wake me up at 7:30 a.m. After I woke up, I was able to determine that I had filled more than 6,000 single-game tickets myself and we printed them that day and our season ticket holders were none the wiser. Moral of the story is, in this business, the only thing that matters is getting the job done no matter what the circumstances!

— Scott Loft, Jacksonville Jaguars

Clearwater Phillies: We had an organist at all our home games, Wilbur Snapp. His name alone is enough to make you laugh. Wilbur played during the breaks between innings. One night we had an absolutely horrible call by the umpire crew and our manager was kicked out for arguing the blatant bad call. Wilbur Snapp reacted like his name —"in a snap" — and began playing "Three Blind Mice," which the umpire did not take too well — so much that he proceeded to stop the game and eject Wilbur Snapp and me as the general manager due to the disrespect the umpire had been shown. I started to argue with the head umpire and then I stopped arguing and I thanked him. His decision to eject Wilbur was perfect — I immediately went to our press box and informed the reporters about what had occurred and went to my office, where I called every local TV station, which immediately sent TV crews; I called USA Today, UPI and AP. Wilbur's ejection was picked up locally, regionally, nationally and even made it internationally.

Paul Harvey, the rest of the story: We received more media requests and coverage than anyone in the Minor League Association had ever heard of. We sold new sponsorships to Disney (the mouse), super markets worked with us to have their names associated with "Let them eat cheese nights" (the league would not allow us to play the song any longer or use the words from "Three Blind Mice," but they could not stop us from taking advantage of the situation to gain unprecedented attention and most importantly garner new revenues!).

— Dave Rowan, Philadelphia Eagles

Paul Bugli, who was my sales executive at ADP, used to always quip, "You Gotta Wanna," meaning you have to want it each and every day to be successful. My second winter working at ADP up in Reading, I had to deal with some unusual circumstances. It was the snowiest winter on record ... it snowed more than 118" that season with temperatures never reaching the freezing mark. It became increasingly difficult to not only make sales appointments, but to just make it out in the field to meet with people. In Reading there was nowhere for the plows to push the snow. You literally could not make it into town, unless you walked. When owners would tell me to wait until spring I would ask them why. They would tell me how the snow was ruining their business and how they couldn't do anything about it. I just told them to expect me no matter what, and that if need be I would help them shovel snow. I just wanted five minutes. Owners were so impressed that a salesperson would walk around town in the snow to meet with them. I ended up killing my quota, because none of the other salespeople were making it out to their appointments. I figured out that I may have been the only sales guy doing door-to-door walking appointments. I just wanted it more than my competitors.

— Scott Stork, Cendant

Just as a negative attitude can bring an organization to its knees, a positive attitude can help lift an organization to unbelievable heights.

When I arrived at ADP-Princeton, the region was known as the Bad News Bears of ADP. In a company that rewards, recognizes and highlights sales performance, the Princeton region was consistently viewed as the laughing stock of the company, finishing the previous year a mere 60% of quota. Only one person had achieved President's Club that year, while most regions had 20 or more.

I knew I was considered a fast rising star at the company — and that is why I was selected and sent to turn around the worst in the country. I wanted to focus on create a winning attitude and that is where I placed my focus for the first 12 months. I did not add products or services, I merely focused on instilling a winning attitude. I channeled all my energy into controllable emotions: enthusiasm, positive reinforcement and the belief that everything was possible.

I knew the smile on my face would be contagious and always pushed people to see the silver lining in every cloud. Pictures of President's Club trips were hung throughout the office. Motivational quotes were e-mailed daily as a constant reminder to reach for the stars. It is amazing what a positive attitude can do for a work force.

— Rich Litt, ADP

ADP-Princeton would become a legendary turnaround story in ADP lore. With Rich on board, ADP-Princeton led the nation in sales and percentage of quota for the next three years.

Life isn't Always Roses

Unfortunately, the chips will not always fall in your favor. It is important to maintain a positive outlook in the face of adversity.

I moved from Philadelphia to Boston in late 1996. This was the third time I had had to pick up and leave my job. I started with my dream job in New York working for the National Basketball Association corporate offices. When I got engaged, I left the NBA for Philadelphia and accepted a job as director of sponsorship services at Global Sports, a company putting on Hoop It Up, 3-on-3 basketball tournaments. While my husband was attending Harvard Business School, I would be the sole breadwinner in the family. It was a two-year program and I would support us by getting a job in the new city.

Finding a job in sports marketing in Boston proved to be a time consuming process. Throughout the job search process, I took temp jobs at various companies in the area for three months prior to finding a job. One day, the parking guard had called in sick, so instead of the usual office work, I spent the day waving cars through the security checkpoint.

— Lisa Reynolds, TOBI Productions

After college and four years of experience in sports marketing, Lisa was forced out of her job and in a new city. The pressure of supporting her husband did not help. She chose to stay positive. Lisa smiled through her misfortune. Only someone with a tremendous sense of humor, self-confidence and positive attitude could laugh about something like this. It could have been very easy for Lisa to be upset and angry at the temp agency, her boss, the absent guard and her husband, but she chose to look at the situation with a positive mental attitude and smile.

The first sales call I did — as the acting general manager of the Peninsula Pilots in the Carolina League (class AA baseball) — was at the local bowling alley to try to sell them an outfield billboard and lucky number program ad. I asked for the general manager and instead of answering in a friendly way, the nice lady behind the counter (I swear this is true) pulled out a shot gun from under the counter and said, "Get the hell out of here before I shoot you in the ass."

I was shaking. I wondered just what kind of region I'd chosen to try to make my living in. When I explained what had happened to the elderly gentleman who looked after our offices, he gave me a sharp look and said, "You went where?" When I told him, the truth came out. He explained to me that the former general manager — the one for who I was acting as replacement— had put the daughter of the lovely lady behind the counter in a "family way," then skipped town. No wonder the nice lady behind the counter was a little sour on the opportunity I was trying to peddle!

I made a mental note about Peninsula Lanes — as you can imagine — but I had already decided that this was going to be a challenge I would surmount. I contacted the former general manager and found out he was not as averse to owning up to his responsibilities as his initial actions might indicate. I then called Peninsula and put the nice lady at the counter in contact with the father of her grandchild. As I hoped, I benefited from the situation: Peninsula became a regular sponsor. More importantly, a family was put back together.

— *Dave Rowan, Philadelphia Eagles*

Identifying Attitude

It becomes very clear, very quickly what kind of attitude you maintain in the workplace. Remember, most jobs you get right out of college will offer you the opportunity to be successful. The differentiating factors will be hard work and attitude. Sending the message of a positive mental attitude may include the following:

- *Smile more.* It lets people know you are happy to be there. Smiling also makes you more approachable. People want to be around happy, positive people. Make yourself one of those people.

- *Be courteous.* Your mother was right. Hold doors for people, let others go ahead of you if there is a line. Be more likable.

- *Act like it is an interview every day.* Be professional, work hard, and respect others' opinions and views.

On a hot and humid day in the middle of July, I took off for my second sales appointment of my young career. I was heading to a health company, called Group Health Insurance of Iowa. Since almost throwing up all over myself and nearly getting thrown out of my first sales call two days earlier, I figured I would get in some much needed practice. So, prior to this appointment, I practiced my "sales pitch" each and every night in front of a mirror. Talk about a lonely feeling … standing in an empty apartment practicing your sales pitch in front of a mirror. Not too glamorous a life for a recent college graduate.

I was ready for this sales call. I was psyched. So, in I went and for the next 15 minutes I tried to explain to the president and CEO of this group health corporation why he and his company needed Quad City Thunder basketball tickets. At the time, I think I actually got better. In hindsight, I proceeded to almost throw up all over myself, again.

However, something different happened this time. Instead of almost getting thrown out of the guy's office like before, the president said something that has stayed with my to this day. He said, "We'll buy." I almost fell out of my chair. I couldn't believe it. He was actually going to buy. We spent the next 15 minutes finalizing the ticket deal.

As he wrote the check, I was interested to find out exactly what I said to make him buy. So, I asked him. I figured I could take this one bit of advice with me on my next sales call. He said the reason he bought from me that day wasn't because they needed Quad City Thunder tickets or because of something I said.

He said the reason he bought was because he could see something in me, which he knew would be successful some day. He could see I was starting out and wanted to provide me with a little nudge in positive energy.

I wouldn't say that I have made millions over the past 12 years, but I can say that I have had a lot of fun and made a pretty good living for me and my family. To me, that is successful. I guess the president of the Group Health Insurance Company knew what he was talking about.

— Dave Cohen, Atlanta Falcons

- Stay away from the negative group. In most organizations there is a group of people who are negative. They feel they are getting the short end of the stick and that life isn't fair to them and consequently would rather look for excuses than bear down and work. This group is often concerned about how much money everyone else makes, who is getting paid overtime and who gets an extra week of vacation. You do not want to be associated with this group. They are usually at the lower levels of the organization and will most likely stay there.

The elevator door opened. Quickly, 10 people filed in on their way back to work from lunch. The last group to enter was four account service co-workers from the largest advertising agency in New England. On my short ride to the 20th floor, I could not help but overhear them berating one of our biggest clients.

Account Executive #1:   "Can you believe what a pain in the ass Dan Thompson is?"

Account Executive #2: "He just doesn't get it — how could they not like any of the creative ideas we presented today — they have no clue!"

Account Executive #3:   " *I wish I could get off this damn account.*"

As the elevator door opened on my floor, the account team paraded off, continuing their loud narrative about how awful "the client" was. As I followed them off the elevator, I noticed a well-dressed older man exit with me. He looked annoyed and in a huge rush.

Less than an hour later, an urgent e-mail from our CEO was sent to the entire agency, which read:

"Our agency philosophy centers around hard work, respect and loyalty to each other and to our clients. With that said, I am deeply troubled by a conversation that was overheard today inside our office by one of our long-standing and most important clients. I hope none of us loses sight of the fact that our clients are the very reason for our success and livelihood as an agency."

The well-dressed older man was the senior vice president/marketing of the account discussed in the elevator. He got off the elevator and marched straight to the CEO's office to relay what he had just heard.

By the way, the assistant account executive got her wish: She was taken off the account … permanently! As the adage goes, if you have nothing nice to say, don't say anything at all.

— *Wendy Eskandarian Arnold, Worldwide*

- *Let your boss know you like your job.* Every once in a while tell your boss, co-workers and clients how happy you are at your job and how fortunate you feel to be part of the organization.

- *Compliment others for a job well done.* People love to be appreciated.

- *Treat everyone as you would the CEO.* Nothing is worse than a brown-noser, a person only pleasant to the top dogs in the organization. Be friendly to everyone, from the janitor to the security guard to the receptionist to the bean counters.

- *Say thanks.* Thank people with a quick note or e-mail when they help you out or go out of their way to make your life easier. Don't underestimate the power of a thank-you note. People enjoy being thanked and are flattered when people go out of their way.

- *Don't talk about your weekend drinking expeditions.* Young people will go out on the town and enjoy themselves. Often times, work will become a social hub and you will hit the town with friends from work. Be careful about having you and your escapades being the hot topics of conversation. Executives might want to live vicariously through you by hearing the stories and even might ask you about them. This type of conversation will frame you as a young party hound. Not exactly what is going to propel you up the corporate ladder. Go out and have fun, but keep the workplace separate.

- *Volunteer for additional projects at work.* Be a team player. It will be recognized and rewarded. Each year at ADP, Eric would volunteer to dress up for the annual Family Christmas Party. Eric as a Power Ranger and Eric as Barney were huge hits with the kids. More importantly, Eric was further appreciated throughout the company by the parents (his co-workers).

- *Change is very difficult for people to accept and enjoy.* Change at work could mean a new boss, getting a new territory, being transferred to a different office, getting new computer software or phone systems. Change represents opportunity for the most active and hardest working. Embrace change and look for ways you can make the change easier for others.

- *Be part of the team.* Participate on the softball team, corporate basketball team and charitable or community events with other members of the organization. Pay special attention if the owner of the company or senior level executives has a certain affinity for a particular event.

- *Attend the holiday party and the summer picnic.* Don't be the drunk that everyone talks about the next day.

- *Work hard and play hard.*

HUMOR

You're probably thinking to yourself, "I am not Chris Rock or Jerry Seinfeld." The great thing about humor is that you do not have to be a comedian. No one is going to send you to a humor workshop, although it probably isn't a bad idea. A humorous disposition will add a lot to your life, as well as to those around you. Laughing is infectious and therapeutic. People will respond well to you if you have a sense of humor.

Be okay with laughing at yourself when you make mistakes, because you will make them. It shows you are comfortable and confident and helps to get others to drop their guard. Eric would often use anecdotal stories with young intimidated sales people when he first became a manager. He would tell stories of having his mother tie his ties in the morning, mismatching his socks and leaving his daily planner on top of his car as he sped down the highway, late to another appointment. By using humor at his own expense, he was able to get his sales people to smile and relax.

Don't tell jokes at the expense of others. Stay away from inappropriate jokes, including but not limited to religious, racist or sexual jokes of any nature. If you follow the general rules of using humor to lift people up, not put people down, you will generally be safe.

Be careful with humor at work if you are not performing at a high level. There is a fine line between being funny and being a clown. (Shoot for funny.) Timing isn't everything, it is the only thing. If you are doing a great job at work, then you will probably have more wiggle room to make jokes on the job. However, when in doubt, save the jokes for a friend at the bar.

> *I have always had the gift of making people laugh. Humor is easy at work — people are tense and situations come up all the time that beg for a quick joke. From practical jokes to my very dry sense of humor and use of timing, it was my way of having fun at work. I had a slow start when I first took my job (actually about 12 months) for my sales to catch up with my sense of humor. I remember the day when I finally became one of the top three achievers in the region, and the vice president commented, "Tom is much funnier when he is performing over plan." Ain't that the truth.*
>
> *— Tom Logio, ADP*

WORK, CAN BE FUN ...

Eric was having a bad day at work and one of his bosses in passing queried, "If it was fun then they wouldn't call it work." Eric thought about that statement through a few sleepless nights and appealing to his positive nature, decided to dispel the notion that work could not be fun. Why can't work be fun? We work too many hours not to have fun.

Millions of people go to work every day and are miserable. Many have the "Sunday Night Blues," dreading Monday in the office. If you do not attack the job like you love it, then you have already lost. Similarly, if you show up to work with a negative feeling about your day, then you really lose. You will spend too much time at work to be miserable. Conversely, if you are positive and enjoying your work, you will perform at a higher level while having fun. You will never achieve greatness in doing something that you do not love. That is where the passion starts.

Thriving on attitude is important to hastening your level of success in your career. Working like you own the company, taking your work personally and bringing your game face to work will help you stand out from the crowd. This approach will lead you along the right path.

WORK AS IF YOU ARE AN OWNER

Treat your company and everything that belongs to your company as if it were your own. There perhaps is nothing worse than watching employees misuse company money or supplies and carry on with the "it is not my money" attitude. Short of a quality assurance lab for a chair manufacturer, no company pays their employees to sit around.

> As an executive of a Fortune 500 Company, I take a lot of pride in managing the company's money as if it were my own. It is a matter of respect. I feel that how my sales managers spent their money is a good indication of what kind of business owners they would be. My experience is that those who can run a tight ship and run their sales team like a business go on to be much more successful than those who just expense everything without regard to its effect on the bottom line. Those who carry an attitude like, "It's not my money," are not usually around too long. I have always treated the company's expense policy for what it is, and nothing enrages me more than reps who abuse their privilege in regards to an expense account.
>
> — Karen Boylan, ADP

Get into the habit of understanding how your decisions affect the company's bottom line. As the owner of a business you must manage both the revenue and cost sides of the business. Early on in a career, young people are often rewarded for delivering either revenue or cutting costs and rarely held accountable for profitability. Recognizing and understanding the business is a good habit to form and it will be recognized down the road.

Chapter 3

Playing the Game

Perception is reality.

— Anonymous

TAKE IT PERSONALLY

Take your work personally and with the utmost pride. Be eager to put out the best work possible. The work you deliver is a manifestation of yourself. Consider all that you do and how it reflects on you and your character. When you show passion for your work, it will spill over into great positive reactions from those around you. Treat every project like your life depended on its success. Approach every day as if it were your last.

BRING YOUR GAME FACE

It is important to bring your zest for life to the office. Often times, people forget who they are and what makes them special outside the office. Bring your personality and energy into the workplace and make work part of your life.

Bob was Mr. Everything in college. He was the type of person everyone liked to be around. He was the life of the party. Bob was involved in more campus activities than anyone in the history of the school. He seemed to have a zest for life that showed through in everything he did. Bob was a tremendous athlete and fierce competitor and hated to lose more than he liked to win. Then the worst thing in the world happened to Bob: He graduated. Life was no longer fun for him. He bounced between four different jobs over the course of his first three years out of school. Nothing seemed to be a "fit" and he became very unhappy. Bob had forgotten what made him special, likeable and successful in college. Bob did not bring his game face to work. To Bob, work was just a job and he got bogged down on an average career path. Bob needed to bring the same passion and energy to work that he carried through college.

A positive attitude will serve you well in work and in life. Too many people do not bring the positive mental attitude to work each day. People want to be around positive people. People want to meet, have lunch with and promote positive people. They are more enjoyable to be around and they make the work environment more pleasant. Be positive — it is the one thing you can always control.

uestion: Do you want to be a player?

Answer: Are you willing to play the game?

You can be in THE job and have the best attitude in the world, but if you don't know the rules of the game you will do poorly at work. Despite popular opinion, work is a game. It is a game where the best do not necessarily win. The smartest, hardest working and most qualified workers are not necessarily those recognized and promoted. To succeed in the workplace, you need to know the rules.

For example, to be successful, it is essential to understand the difference between "out of the box" thinking and being a renegade. Corporations want you to be coachable, but not a robot. You must learn to manage perceptions and proactively dictate how others will perceive you. This chapter will teach you the rules and provide tips to make you more effective in positively positioning yourself in the eyes of the organization's top executives.

LEARN FROM WATCHING, ASKING QUESTIONS AND LISTENING

Whatever your grade or position, if you know how and when to speak, and when to remain silent, your chances of real success are proportionately increased.
— *Ralph C. Smedley*

When you start your job, you will most likely want to jump right in and start running full speed. Who could blame you? It is exciting and you are anxious to prove yourself and be successful. A young person entering the work force is like an air conditioning system in a car. Have you ever gotten into your car on a hot and humid summer day and blasted the air conditioner to try to cool off? The result is piping hot air that makes you perspire even more. Eventually, the air becomes cooler and you keep it going full blast until you have ice cycles hanging from your eyebrows. By the time you find the happy medium, you have already arrived at your destination.

A successful career is more a marathon than a sprint. Early on in a job, it is essential to spend time watching, asking questions and listening to determine where emphasis will need to be placed. Be patient and let the car warm up before you turn on the air conditioner.

At a fast growing technology and service company, I was asked to run one of our small business units as a general manager. There were about six of us all running different business units or sectors. Our mutual boss was a very strong leader and powerful personality in the company. He liked to create a competitive atmosphere between the general managers of these business units by actively pointing out what the others were doing well, etc. Through a combination of hard work and luck, my business unit began to prosper and grow much faster than any other business units. I had used an "us against the world" approach to motivate my young team and they responded beautifully. It was not uncommon to share news about major customer wins through communications with the entire company. We had a particularly good streak of success and I began sending out messaging promoting our group to the rest of the company.

While my team responded enthusiastically, I laid it on a little too thick and created some resentment among my peers running other business units. What I didn't understand (until my boss explained it to me) was that the only way to be promoted was for my peers to work for me. I had been so competitive and intent on charging up my team that I failed to realize how my behavior had created resentment toward me by my peers. This put my boss in a tough situation and probably cost me a promotion.

— Jaime Smith, FreeMarkets

Human nature plays a big role in determining our reactions to situations. When nervous, excited or anxious, we speak too much, out of turn, act too quickly or slowly, and forget to experience and take in what is happening around us. Often times this leads to a reactive response. Our goal is to help you become more proactive. The first step is becoming an active listener who asks questions and follow-up questions. It is imperative to concentrate on listening. Do not think of another question when the person is answering the first question asked. Be interested and soak up the information. Active listening will provide better insight into understanding the people and surrounding work environment.

It was evident at the New Jersey Nets that sales were the major focus on the business side of the organization. Most pro sports teams have two sales groups: tickets and sponsorships. By talking to the ticket sales people and scheduling meetings with the sponsorship group, Scott quickly learned that the sponsorship sales group was more highly regarded than the ticket sales group. How did he know this? Indications were throughout the organization, as the sponsorship sales people were in offices, while the ticket sales people were in cubicles. That was the easy part. But the true answers became clear when Scott began to ask questions.

> *I spent the first few months just listening: to stories, anecdotes, experiences, and the importance of industry contacts of which I had very few. The sponsorship people had contacts with everyone in the market including the other pro teams' executives. If anyone needed anything, from a new car deal to free cameras for an event, the sponsorship guys got the call. Clearly, those were the players with the power and exactly where an upcoming guy would want to be. The sponsorship people were also paid significantly more than the ticket sales people were, which is never a bad thing.*

> *I knew I had a choice to make. The sponsorship group was old school, middle-aged career Nets employees. It was a closely knit, guarded group that dressed well, lived and died with the team, hated the Knicks and shunned outsiders. The ticket sales people were young (like me), inexperienced (like me), and open to new ideas (like me) and trying to find a way — any way — to be successful (like me). Unfortunately, they were not regarded in the industry or organization as power players. I knew I could be successful quicker in the ticket sales group. But, I knew that careers are marathons, not sprints. It was much more important to listen and learn.*

> *I realized that if there were a way to get into the sponsorship sales group, I would be at a tremendous competitive advantage over the 25 people my age selling tickets. The first seven months were spent as an assistant in the sponsorship group at the Nets trying to gain the respect and confidence of the sponsorship group, as well as other executives who would determine my future at the team. I aligned myself with the sponsorship group, eventually being promoted to sponsorship sales, which launched my career.*

> *— Scott M. O'Neil*

SEEK TO UNDERSTAND

What makes successful people successful? What can you do as an employee to make them happy? What actions should you avoid that will upset them? What is your boss's personal mission statement? Do you understand the department goals? Company goals? Do you have a clear set of expectations and the goals laid out for you? You need to find the answers to these questions. Proactively searching out what you need to do to be successful is imperative. Seek to understand what motivating and determining success factors exist at your workplace. They are often different from company to company and the answers will not be found in the employee handbook.

KNOW THE COMPANY

The more you know about your company, the more effective you will be. Understand and know your company's history inside and out. Be aware of everything — from understanding who founded the company and the history of the CEOs, right down to the sales from last year. Include in your knowledge your company's biggest competitor and know everything about that company as well. Study your company and learn from its past. Surf the Web and visit the library to research the past. There is also the opportunity to ask the "old timers" in the office for their thoughts on the past, present and future. Most "old timers" will be flattered and provide insights beyond any you could find staring into the computer screen.

Know the competition as if you were preparing to fight them in battle. As a matter of fact, make a game of it to keep it fun. The world is as big as you make it. If you merely live and breath inside your company's walls then that is all you know. However, the more knowledge and information you have about the market, competitors, suppliers, distributors, strategic partners, etc., the better equipped you will be to understand the direction the company is going and your role within it.

THE SUCCESS PATH

Destiny is not a matter of chance, it is not a matter of choice; it is not a thing to be waited for, it is a thing to be achieved.
— *W.J. Bryan*

It is important to understand where you want to go within your organization. Many times workers and employees show up and even work a hard day. Unfortunately, that is usually not enough. If you do not know where you want to go, you will never arrive at the next destination. By understanding your company and what other employees do, you can develop an idea of where you want to go. Is your boss's job one you would aspire to? If so, find out how he got there and what it takes to make it to the next level.

Many people never take the time to get a history of the people to whom they are reporting. It is important to know something about each boss you have all the way up the ladder to the CEO. What college did they attend? How long have they been at the company? Are they married? Do they have children? Be aware of diplomas hanging in offices and pictures on desks. Be aware. At the very least, it will provide a conversation piece on line at the company picnic. At best, the information will help you navigate through the corporate bureaucracy.

In school (college) I, like every other student, asked myself the inevitable questions: What do I want to be? What do I want to do with the rest of my life? On a deeper level what I want to be would determine what I wanted to do. But how many 18-year-olds have any idea of what they are doing on a Friday night let alone for the rest of their lives? To answer this question as a freshman I knew the first priority was grades and understanding the new freedom of college. And that's what I did — no clubs or organizations until I was comfortable with school as it applied to the work. After that was established it was time to get involved.

My sophomore year at Villanova, I came out gunning. If I wanted to figure out what I wanted to do I needed to try things. I got my hand in everything I could. New student orientation, intramural sports, hall counsel, I even drove an ambulance! However, when you get involved with a lot of "things" you figure out what you like but more importantly what you don't like. During this search I found the organization that, as it turns out, was the foundation of my career path.

The Villanova Sports Marketing Association was comprised of 12 students with an advisor who assisted the actual marketing department with promotions at football and basketball games, and marketed all other sports at Villanova. This group made me realize very quickly where the fun was — sports.

When I found the group that made me happy I went with it full force to try and learn as much as I could. When the members of the marketing staff realized I was serious about getting involved I found they were serious about making that happen. Soon I was fully involved, executing on-court promotions, telemarketing, and occasionally being invited to staff meetings.

My first staff meeting was one of the biggest learning experiences of my life. Not so much because of the content of the meeting but because I began to understand the importance of acting like a professional. In this meeting there were two members of the Philadelphia Eagles sales staff. Coincidentally one of them has been the most important person in my professional life.

Unfortunately, I showed up to this meeting 20 minutes late with my (at the time) wild hair and in sandals. I came into a room with six or eight people in suits dressed to kill. And there I was looking like I was going to a barbecue! That was my first look into the corporate world and it was also the first time I realized how much work I needed to make it in sports.

As time went on I cleaned up my act, got a hair cut and even bought some nice shoes. I also became very close with the staff. I found the harder I worked and more time I spent there, the more they involved me with what they were working on. It may have been as simple as listening to a sales call but it all had meaning and there was something to learn from each thing I was exposed to.

Eventually, we transformed the association into a real support unit of the actual marketing staff. The association took some of the pressure off their marketing the Olympics sports so they could focus more of their time on basketball and football. We developed and executed full marketing plans, which was invaluable experience for us but also a great help to a staff that was already spread thin.

All these experiences in my college days came full circle during my senior year when I walked into the first day of my sports marketing class only to see the very same person from the Philadelphia Eagles teaching the class. The class, like no other, focused not on theory but on the real question: "How can I make it in sports?" What can I do to make it happen? (Which coincidently has become my mantra.) Anything can happen, you just need to know how to "make it happen." This phrase has become very important to me because as I have discovered, no one wants to hear excuses. People want things done. You need to learn how to make it happen regardless of what you are doing.

As the class progressed I would see this professor and we would chat at games and other events. Little did I know what this relationship would mean later. It was graduation time and I, like many students, had lots of interviews and even an offer or two but doing what? I thought I found a potential job selling TV advertising — sounded great; no money, lots of hours but potential. After a few weeks, I could see it wasn't going to pan out and I picked up a temporary job watering trees. I was given a tractor and 500 gallons of water and told, "Keep these trees alive." Great! I have a college degree and I am a water boy!

One very hot day I get a call from a member of the sports marketing department a Villanova. I will never forget his quote: "Scott O'Neil has taken a job working for the NBA and needs an assistant. You interested in the spot?" Needless to say, it was the easiest question I have ever had to answer. "Of course," I told him.

The very next day I called that member of the Eagles sales staff, that professor I had at Nova — Scott O'Neil... and it began to happen. I had never been to New York before, never taken mass transit, never done any big city things, but here I was going to NYC to interview with the NBA. After a few interviews I was offered the job. No place to live and a limited wardrobe — but I had a job and not only a job but a job working for one of the biggest leagues in the world!

Any job can become frustrating. One day I got a call from the TV sales job that I had been waiting for — I had been in the professional world for two months, and I was actually thinking about switching until I had a chat with Scott, who promptly straightened me out. Why give up the NBA and sports for TV sales? Potential to make a lot of money? I could not really answer the question. He told me, "It's your call, do what you want, but you're 21 and working for the NBA." He was right. It wasn't going to happen over night, but there was no better place to start than where I was.

To be continued....

— Jim Corson, NBA

Information and awareness are the key factors enabling you to effectively communicate with the higher-ups. When you understand the whole picture, you will obtain a tremendous edge. In other words, do not ask the CEO how things are going if the stock price just hit an all-time low.

I did an internship with Palace Sports & Entertainment during the summer of 1996. Before I was finished I sat down and spoke with "Giz" about further career opportunities. He mentioned the entry level ticket sales department (outside sales) as an option for me upon my graduation. I told him that I was unsure if I wanted to sell, but was willing to try. I was heading into my senior year at Ohio University and we had a six-week break for the holidays. I asked Giz if I could come up and sell for those six weeks to decide if it was something I thought I could do. He agreed to pay me $150 per week plus commissions. I accepted and moved up to Detroit the Friday after Thanksgiving. Keep in mind I only had six weeks, so I didn't have much time.

The first week I spent cold calling and I loved it. I loved the challenge of getting decision makers on the phone and selling them. Going into week two, I realized that I'd be better off trying to sell people off of the incoming line because people kept telling me to call them after the holidays. By then I would be in back in Athens, Ohio, so I had to have a plan B. This is when I started to train myself how to upsell. People would call in for a game and I'd sell them four. We had a buy-three-get-one-free promotion going.

I started selling these like crazy. What I didn't know was that there was a contest going. Whoever sold the most four-packs got a trip on the team plane to the All-Star Game. In January, after my stint in Detroit was completed I got a phone call from my supervisor from December. He read me an e-mail that he had sent to the entire sales staff. I'm paraphrasing here, so bear with me. "Congratulations to Glen Kwiatowski for winning the four-pack contest. He will be enjoying the All-Star Game. There was also another rep whom I cannot remember (that was me) who was second."

He then stated that everyone below number three should be ashamed of themselves because a college kid who worked for a month kicked all of their asses. This contest ran from October through January and I almost won it in a month. This was the moment when I realized that I could be good at this and sales was where I would have a career.

— Doug Dawson, Indiana Pacers

Interview The Boss.

What a strange, yet essential concept! Fortunately, most people are flattered when you show this kind of interest in them. This will allow relatively easy access and information.

I can remember this like it was yesterday. I scheduled a meeting with my boss, Scott Taroff, to talk about the future. I asked him numerous questions about his career goals and expectations of our sales group. Understanding his goals allowed me access others did not have. I now had *a better feel regarding his decisions and actions. I got the feeling that Taroff knew I understood his goals and would often approach me with a new idea or plan he was about to roll out and ask my opinion as to how to best lay this out to the rest of the troops. He often commented that his comfort level came from our mutual understanding of where the organization was heading and where it needed to go.*

— Eric J. Hinds

Prepare yourself for situations you anticipate will arise. For example, find out the lunchtime topic of conversation and contribute accordingly. If the topic is the short-term bond market, get up an extra hour early each day and read the *Wall Street Journal*. If it is NBA basketball, watch "SportsCenter." The key is to be interested before you are interesting.

The top two sponsorship sales people at the Nets talked about three things: Nets basketball, New York football (one liked the Jets, the other the Giants) and college basketball. These were easy topics for Scott, because they were also interests of his. Play the game and don't be too pigheaded and stubborn. Ask others' opinions about their topics of interest, but be careful with your opinions. Work is not your open forum for controversial topics. Avoid discussing politics, religion and sex at all costs.

GROUP THINK

In every organization, different groups of people exist: the leaders, the doers, the movers and shakers, the climbers, the complainers, the slackers, the flower pots and the fast trackers. The groups are rarely clear cut and often times there are crossovers. The group you are associated with will dictate how people respond to you, how people see you and how fast you will climb in an organization. Decide what group you want to be associated with and make the effort to fit in that group.

Doers. These people do their jobs. They are not looking for attention, fanfare or accolades. These people work hard and are usually concerned about keeping the current job. These people are risk averse and avoid conflict and confrontation at all costs. These people are not normally promoted quickly, but are valuable in every organization. Make friends with these people. Example: ADP is a 50-year old organization that was built on processing payroll. The driving force is sales, but the backbone is the operational group. The operations group at ADP is full of doers. They have low turnover and high loyalty and commitment to the organization.

Movers and Shakers. This group of people likes to mix it up. They are usually involved in and around the action. They normally are found in the most respected and desired part of the organization. The members are extremely confident and like to hook their wagons to the number one horse. There are not too many of these people with the gold watch for 25 years of dedicated service.

> When I was an intern in my junior year in college I was assigned to pick up the consultant working for our company. Normally, whoever was around to pick up the consultant was chosen. Pretty random. On my first trip to the airport with this guy I really enjoyed him. He was super smart and was about to revamp the organization I was interning for. When I got back to the office I told the intern director, who was a non-motivated, just give me a paycheck type person, that I'd like to be the one to pick him up every time he comes in. After my request, which was granted, the intern director used to embarrass me all the time that I was a brown-nose to this guy and everyone around me would laugh. For awhile I stayed away from the consultant to cobble favor with the rest of the people who were laughing at me. Then it hit me. All of the people who were laughing were all average employees, no superstars among them. I thought, "What am I, crazy?" I went back to spending time with the consultant for the rest of my internship. Fast forward one year and this consultant hired me to work at the team out of college. Four years later, all those people laughing at me were working for me! Good thing I chose to ignore the peer pressure to just be average.

> — Howie Nuchow, Mandalay Sports and Entertainment

Complainers. Nothing is ever good enough for the members of this group. Members of this group always feel they are getting screwed. "Life isn't fair" is the group's mantra. Complainers often find it easier to complain than to work. New projects are usually met with immediate resistance and disdain. They are usually bitter and can rarely find happiness with someone else's success. Remember, cancer spreads — stay away!

9 to 5ers. Oddly enough, these people work from 9:00 a.m. to 5:00 p.m. and not a second longer. Nine to 5ers view work as necessary evil to pay the bills. They are not necessarily negative, but are rarely positive. Members of this group are often time-oriented as opposed to goal oriented.

Slackers. Slackers usually act alone and avoid groups. These people will do anything to avoid work. Slackers can be found at the water cooler, reading the paper, chatting about the previous night's escapade or just about anything to put off starting the workday.

Slackers are usually friendly and may even have good rapport with the boss. Slackers are dreamers, sometimes lazy and often times bright. Slackers do not want to do the things winners are willing to do.

Flower Pots. This group represents the career employees. They long for the days when employees worked for the same company for their entire lives. This group is happy with the status quo and always fights change. Example: Older stock brokers represent the quintessential flowerpots. As the industry moves to on-line trading, many brokerage houses are positioning them as financial consultants and away from day trading. These employees have worked for one brokerage house for years and are insistent on merely trading stocks and complaining about the coming changes. Despite the constant struggle, they are career employees.

Fast Trackers. This group is filled with potential superstars who don't have a problem putting them above the organization. This is a group on the rise. The members are usually willing to take the first job offer if it means moving up the ladder at a quicker pace. This group sees the big picture and wants a bigger piece of the pie. This is a group that believes in the philosophy of "Up or Out."

Ask yourself who you want to be and how you want to be perceived. Look around and see what group you have attached yourself to and decide if that is where you want to be.

FINDING A MENTOR

Very few men are wise by their own counsel, or learned by their own teaching. For he that was only taught by himself had a fool for his master.
— *Ben Johnson*

One key to success in the rat race is finding a quality mentor. Finding a good mentor is one of the most difficult, yet important tasks you must take on early in your career. A mentor is someone you respect who can help you with advice along the many stumbling blocks and road bumps you will hit along your path up the corporate ladder. It is not normally a formal relationship. There is nothing in writing, any formal contract or written rules. It is merely a mutual understanding and respect between two people.

A mentor should be someone comfortable with his position, who won't feel threatened by you and will enjoy seeing and contributing toward your successes. More progressive companies now have formalized mentor programs, which are fantastic opportunities. It is equally important to give back to your mentor. Speak highly of the person and give credit when it is due. Send the person a holiday card, get the person a birthday cake or send flowers. Let the person know that it is not wasted time.

Recognize that people are willing help you in your career, although you will need to be proactive and ask for help. Most likely, the person you have targeted will be flattered and take you up on the opportunity. Make the mentor someone to whom you will have access and someone who will be willing to spend time with you.

How Can You Find A Mentor(s)?

Unfortunately, there is no magic formula to finding the perfect mentors. Remember not to limit yourself to one person. The more people willing to aid in your development and success, the better off you will be. Some places to be on the lookout for prospective mentors:

     a. Internships

     b. Speakers who come to your university

     c. Professors

     d. Parents

     e. Clients

     f. Bosses (be careful with this one)

Is A Mentor a Role Model?

**People seldom improve when they have
no other model but themselves to COPY.**
— *Oliver Goldsmith*

Recognize the difference between a role model and a mentor. David Stern, the commissioner of the National Basketball Association and recognized around the world as the best sports marketer of his time, is an excellent role model. But Scott did not have access to David Stern, so choosing him as a mentor was both unrealistic and counter-productive. It is important to have both an internal mentor (in same company, division, and plant) and an external mentor (outside the company, but within the industry).

Jon Spoelstra is renowned in the field of sports marketing, an author and turnaround specialist with an affinity for young people who have the will and desire to be successful. Jon was named president and COO of the New Jersey Nets six months after Scott had started with the team. Jon spent time with all the young people, but selected a few "Young Turks" that he would groom.

Scott was one of those few, and to this day, not quite sure how he was chosen. It might be that he was there at 7:30 a.m. each morning making calls, setting up appointments and doing whatever else Jon recommended. Jon once called the young sales people into a room and announced, "This is a tough business. Not all of you will stay in sports marketing and only two, maybe three of you will make it to a vice president level at a team." That was all Scott needed to set another goal. Jon was stretching everyone willing to be stretched. He spent time with the Turks. Jon offered to go on appointments with them (imagine the president of a $100 million company going out on a sales call with a 22-year-old kid). They would go out to a sports bar to watch Nets away games and would sit and talk sports marketing philosophy until the wee hours in the morning, rarely glancing at the television. Jon took mentoring seriously and so did those who were the beneficiaries.

Scott's boss from his Advantage International internship became his external mentor. Bruce Schilling has been a major player in the sports marketing world for more than 20 years. He has always reached out to help Scott along the way and relishes the fact that Scott refers to him as his mentor. The sports industry is small. Everyone seems to know or at least know of everyone. It helps to have someone speaking highly of you in the marketplace. Bruce also got Scott his interview (and big break) at the Philadelphia Eagles. A mentor's purpose is not to get you a job, but they can help lead the horse to water on occasion. External mentors can often provide objective advice about a particular situation (boss, client, how to ask for a raise, etc.). External mentors are usually much less clouded by the politics of the situation and are a good source of information, feedback and advice.

Being a Good Protégé

> The most important single influence in the life of a person
> is another person ... who is worthy of emulation.
> — *Paul D. Schafer*

How can you be a good protégé to keep the relationship strong and productive? Professor Herminia Ibarra at the Harvard Business School has done extensive research on power and influence tactics and mentor and protégé relationships. Professor Ibarra offers the following tips for being a good protégé:

a. Be loyal and dependable.

b. Take every opportunity to make the mentor look good.

c. Become and demonstrate you are interested and passionate about learning.

d. Do more than you are asked.

e. Open yourself up to honesty.

f. Recognize and make the mentor aware that you understand the risks the mentor takes for you.

g. Give as much as you can get.

h. Use the mentor's time and resources selectively.

i. The onus is on you to manage the relationship.

j. Add value to the mentor through your relationships.

DRINKING ON THE JOB

I was working at the New Jersey Festival of Ballooning as the director of sales and marketing. My boss, Howard Freeman, set a sales goal for me that if I hit a certain gross sales number by a certain date, he would allow me to join him at a big industry sponsorship conference called the IEG Sponsorship Seminar. This is the biggest industry shindig where all the leaders in sponsorship gather for three days of information sharing and networking in Chicago, Ill. Howard was one of the featured speakers at the conference on the second morning of the conference. After the first day of meetings and mingling, we went out for some drinks and dinner with a bunch of conference attendees. Howard ducked out early, but I stayed out very late with a group of people and drank heavily. The next morning Howard (my boss, who paid for this trip for me) was scheduled to speak at

9:30 a.m. I woke up the next morning at 10:30 a.m. and missed the entire speech. To this day, more than 10 years later, he has not let me forget that incident.

Moral of the story, don't lose control in any business situation.

— *Andrew Klein, Revolution Marketing*

Be Coachable

Is there anyone so wise as to learn from the experience of others?
— *Voltaire*

Young people in the workplace who are driven to succeed and looking for every advantage to get to the top are often times moving so fast they get pretty high on themselves. It is an easy trap to fall into. Your first job probably will not be brain surgery. Entry level jobs can be met with solid success by working hard, keeping a good attitude and paying special attention to detail.

Jack Start was a high-powered general manager at ADP. He was the man and well respected by everybody in the organization. He cared about people and went out of his way to make people feel good about themselves. In fact, Jack bought the entire management staff a copy of Stephen Covey's book, "Seven Habits of Highly Effective People" I respected Jack and wanted to spend more time with him. However, it was just not realistic to expect a GM to spend time with a sales rep. So, I went out of my way to get to know him ... the Christmas party, company picnics, sales meetings ... whatever it took. I made it clear to him that I respected his opinion and wanted his advice on a number of issues. As I began to reach a level of success, my access to Jack began to increase and so did our relationship. I was always courteous and sent thank-you cards to let him know I was appreciative of his advice. I tried very hard to be coachable.

— *Eric J. Hinds*

As you meet these successes along the way, don't forget to be coachable. Let people help you. Be open and proactively receptive to feedback. If your boss is the one doing the coaching, pay special attention. No matter how smart you think you are or how well you think you are doing, there are people in the organization and community who can and will help if you open up to being coachable.

In the Eagles locker room there is a quote that reads "There is someone getting better at your position today." You can always improve and learn more. Be smart and accept feedback and coaching. There is someone working harder and smarter right on your tail. Do not slow down and do not get caught.

BE CAREFUL OF THE WITCH AND THE WICKED

**Keep away from people who try to belittle your ambitions.
Small people always do that, but the really great make
you feel that you, too can be really great.**
— Mark Twain

Do not let them bring you down. These people often initially disguise themselves as friends and they are not. Others will "dis" you from the beginning and you will spend hours and energy trying to get them to like you.

I had been working at a research contracting firm in Washington, D.C., for about three months when I had a run-in with some fellow researchers. My philosophy on the importance of befriending co-workers was severely challenged by this experience and led me to change my strategy. The misunderstanding took place over the use of a conference room, which I had signed out so I could conduct an interview, but which was used by the "in crowd" to gather and eat lunch. I naively assumed that related activities would take priority over socializing, and asked them to clear the room about 15 minutes before they usually might. Not only did they refuse, but they actually taunted me about needing a few more minutes. I had to go make apologies to my interviewee and only on my third trip back to the room did I find it tidy and vacant.

Needless to say, I looked forward to getting my revenge on the two ring leaders by informing my supervisor of their unprofessional and discourteous conduct. However, to my horror, my supervisor had already been told by the miscreants themselves, and further, sided with them! She tried to explain the importance of learning the culture of the work place and how being social with co-workers allows one to avoid the type of situation I had found myself in that afternoon. I had a very good relationship with my supervisor and so felt very betrayed by her handling of the event. However, after some time had passed (and I stopped mentally throwing daggers at certain people each time I passed them in the hallway), I absorbed the wisdom of what she had to say. Most of us are not at work to make friends, but one should never underestimate how social connections can grease the wheels of professional life.

— *Jean DeBlezza, grad student at FUQUA*

Spend time with those people who will believe in you, help you and want to see you succeed. Do your best to spend the majority of your time with those who care. Do not get emotional or take it personally if you hear the bitterness of some or feel the jealousy of others. The price of being a successful person is that often times there are people in the organization who will not like you. Take the high road and "kill them with kindness."

Keep It Real

Do not be a poser. Dress the part, yes. Act the part, yes. Be coachable, yes. But keep it real. No one likes a fake person and most people can see right through you. You must be sincere and strong in your convictions. Although communication with your boss is crucial to your success, make the conversation about quality and not quantity. Avoid the label of being the brown-noser. It will significantly affect your relationship with your peers and no bosses like, respect or enjoy the company of a brown-noser. Be yourself. Be who you are and do your best to maximize your potential and the chips will generally fall your way.

To reach the top of the corporate ladder it takes determination, hard work and a little bit of good fortune. Identify and focus energy on the type of person you want to be and how you want to be perceived and take steps accordingly. To climb quicker and be more efficient and be perceived in the right light you must play the game and play to win.

Dressing the Part

When in Rome, do as the Romans do.
— *Anonymous*

A rule of thumb at work: dress as the executives dress. Search out the executive people and take notice of how they dress. If the successful people are wearing three button suits, cuff links and striped shirts, you should be wearing three button suits, cuff links and striped shirts. If the bosses are wearing khakis and T-shirts, do the same.

HOW CAN I AFFORD THOSE CLOTHES?

When you are starting a job right out of college, few people have discretionary money to spend on nice clothes. However, your career cannot afford you to dress your age. Be creative and proactive. Use your graduation money for clothes, ask for graduation presents to be suits, shoes, shirts, etc. Ask for work clothes for gifts for the holidays and birthdays. It is important to be a smart shopper. Go to the outlets near you and look twice as nice for half the price. Learn brand names and look for deals. They are out there, you just have to find them. If you do not have the inclination or desire to identify and shop for nice clothes, find someone who does. Believe it or not, some people actually like to shop and will be glad to escort you to the mall.

> *Be neat and professional. People will respect you more if you have it together. For men it is the shoes, belt and tie. Match your shoe and belt color always. Spend the extra time polishing your shoes and make them shine. Always be prepared. I can remember spilling orange juice on my shirt and tie as I tried to eat as I drove to work. My boss lent me his extra shirt he had hanging behind his door. I have had an extra shirt, tie and jacket at work ever since.*

> — *Eric J. Hinds*

LEARNING THE LESSON THE HARD WAY

Sometimes the hardest lessons to learn are the ones you never forget.

> *As an intern for Advantage International, a sports marketing firm in the Washington, D.C., area, I learned a powerful lesson about appropriate office attire the hard way. The first week of the internship, I entered the hallowed halls of the posh Georgetown office dressed in khakis and a button down shirt, neither of which were dry cleaned (or even ironed) and a roommate's tie. One of the execs (and future boss, mentor and friend), Bruce Schilling, was apparently having a bad day, or at least wanted to send a message and he let me have it. The executive berated me in front of eight staff members and the entire intern crew. It went something like this:*

> Bruce: *"Do you know how much it costs to get a shirt dry cleaned?*

> Scott: *"No, I don't."*

Chapter 4

Time is on Your Side

You must have a plan of action.

— Nadine Hinds

Bruce: *"Obviously. It costs $1. Is that too high a price to pay for looking professional? Huh? We have clients through here every day. This is not the way I want this place represented. This isn't a fraternity party. Are we clear?"*

Scott: *"Well, uh ..."*

Bruce: *"Your belt doesn't even match your shoes. Who taught you to dress, Ray Charles?"*

Everybody within earshot was laughing, except for me. I could feel the heat rushing through my body and my face getting more red by the second. I had 101 smart-alec comments on the tip of my tongue ready to unleash, which I fortunately kept to myself. It did not take me long to clean my act up. I took the abrasive lashing for what it was: good sound advice. I learned about dry cleaning that summer, because I took that VP's shirts to the dry cleaner's each week.

I also learned the importance placed on how you look in the office. For better or worse, perception is reality. If you are dressed slovenly, it will be assumed your work is slovenly.

— Scott M. O'Neil

This is not the best way to deliver a message, or to receive one, but it did make an impact and serve its point. Fortunately, Scott didn't write the guy off as a jerk; ironically the VP to this day is his role model. His name is Bruce Schilling and he is a big shot for NIKE. Bruce was very helpful as a reference in getting Scott's first job and helped him land his second. Bruce is a good, straightforward and honest voice of reason and has provided considerable, quality advice throughout Scott's career.

Much has been taught, written and developed on time management, because it is essential to the success of people in business. This chapter provides some tools you must have as well as a step-by step process to get you organized and on the right track to maximizing your time at work.

FAILING TO PLAN IS PLANNING TO FAIL

Prior planning prevents poor performance.
— *Jim Maltese Sr., Merrill Lynch*

Failure: This still eats at me from time to time. I was in business school and chairman of a committee called Athletes for Charity. The basic idea was to raise money for Special Olympics through a variety of fund raising events, mostly athletics ("for the kids," as we used to say). The goal was to hand Special Olympics a check for $10,000 to $15,000 at the end of the year. We had one major event each semester. First semester it was a golf tournament that went great and we raised about $7,000, so we were in good shape. Spring semester's event was an outdoor concert. We've got great bands lined up, and everything was in place. The only concern was that we weren't able to get a backup indoor venue secured because of scheduling conflicts, so we really needed good weather.

Well, it was a concern, but I said screw it, we don't really have any other options, and we'll be fine. For the two weeks leading up to it, it's about 75 and sunny every day. On the day of the show, it pissed down rain from 6 a.m. to 8 p.m. then it was 75 and sunny for the next week. We got about 75 people to show up (were expecting about 1,200), and lost $11,000 on the day — for the kids. It was the end of the year, so we scrambled to put on a couple of other events to try to cover our losses, but there just wasn't enough time. We ended up having to go to the business school board to ask them for a check just to be able to pay our vendors. It was humiliating.

— Dan Hanlon, Red Level

Overall, life is not fair. People get hired because of a family friend or a contact in the business. Promotions are often doled out based on seniority, and layoffs occur even when a company posts record-breaking profits. Sometimes it is a wonder how anyone is ever successful. Fortunately, life has an equalizer — time. Everyone is given a 24-hour day, a seven-day week, and a 365-day calendar each year. You have the same time in a day as Donald Trump, Michael Dell, Michael Bezos, Bill Gates, and Warren Buffet have to work with each day. The key is to properly budget and maximize your time through careful and continual planning.

Today's business environment is moving at a torrid pace. Ideas, situations, problems and opportunities are continually presented to you without regard to your time, preparedness or willingness to handle them. Simply fielding the situations as they arise merely keeps you afloat and rarely allows a chance for you to catch your breath, plan and get ahead. Time has become the scarcest and most valuable resource in the business world. If you want to accomplish all that you can in the day, week and year, then you must learn how to maximize your time. So as you enter that first big day to set the world on fire with all your ideas and energy, it is important the basics are covered.

Why Organizing and Prioritizing Are Important

80% of a task is done in the planning stage.
— Jeffrey Piluso

Organizing and prioritizing with good time management are skills that must be sharpened in order to thrive in the business world. Being organized is having a system to function seamlessly throughout the day, minimizing surprises and eliminating stress based on confusion. An organized person calls ahead for directions when going on a meeting and files them for a later date. An organized person can pull out notes from a meeting six months ago in a moment's notice and will not have a problem filling out an expense report because all of the receipts are clearly marked and in their proper place. Some people are more disposed to being organized than others are. However, if you are not one of these people, it is something you must focus time and energy on in the near future. Fortunately, there are a number of tools currently available to make you more efficient.

> The thing that was the hardest to learn when I was young in my career was how to prioritize and manage my time. I was overwhelmed with multiple projects and found myself working 12-hour days many times. I was also trying to do so much at once that I would sometimes make mistakes in my work. Since I was trying to get everything done on time I would not double check my work before I distributed it. Through experience, feedback and management I was able to figure out which tasks were urgent and which ones could be pushed aside. It also allowed me to focus on the quality of my work instead of the quantity. One boss in particular pushed me to be better and

focus on quality work by often pointing out my mistakes. At the time I felt that I was being picked on but in the long run it really helped me pay attention to the details in my work and indirectly probably helped me attain the position I have today.

— *Colleen Duffy, ANC Sports*

"Nonsense," you are thinking. "I have never had a problem before, not at previous jobs or even college," you say. Want a shock? Taking orders at the local burger place and making photocopies in the local law office have not properly prepared you. I am sure the strenuous 16-hour college week filled with those grueling 9:30 a.m. m/w/f classes was handled with few problems as well. The alarm goes off at 9:00 a.m., you snooze until 9:20 a.m., then throw a baseball cap on and hustle to class, sliding into the back row just before the professor kicks things off. A syllabus, notebook for each class, and at least one good friend you could call on in case you overslept was all you needed to stay organized and on top of the game in college. That was the minor leagues — welcome to the majors.

Prioritizing is the process of ranking your tasks in order of importance. Internships rarely require much in the form of prioritization. There are rarely multiple tasks to accomplish and when there are, there is usually direction as to which to do first. College has a very structured class schedule. This, combined with an inordinate amount of free time, often eliminates the challenge of prioritization. The real world is about choices. You cannot accomplish everything that you hope to each and every day. Customers will change their minds, offices have emergencies, and the boss's priorities change. Still, you must be prepared to react to all that change and not lose focus of what is important to you. Without a good system of organization and prioritizing, you will be less effective, less efficient and less valuable to your organization.

"ELEPHANT HUNTING"

My early days in the life insurance industry were fraught with tedium and disappointment. So much of your success as a young agent — once you get past the low-hanging fruit that are your friends and relatives — is dependent on your ability to convince perfect strangers to spend several hours with you at their kitchen table, sharing there innermost dreams and concerns all culminating with asking them to give you $1,200/year or more on the promise that you will return it to their family 1,000 fold once they are dead. Few are so selfless, most are uninformed, all are at least skeptical!

I soon figured out that this was not nearly as sexy or engaging as I had imagined. I had endured four years of university for this? This was not high finance, this was not BIG business, this was not an "entrepreneurially spirited pursuit," as had been so eloquently suggested to me by my hiring manager during the recruitment process. Make no mistake — this was my career nightmare and everything my friends said it was going be and worse.

I had all at once morphed into the financial service equivalent of a used car salesman! I needed a way out of this grind. My solution — I was going to be a "corporate pension/benefits specialist." Important meetings, mahogany boardrooms, CEOs with business issues — that was my future. No longer would I toil at the kitchen table of middle-income Canada. I was to take my rightful place on Bay Street, in the heart of Toronto's business district and stake my claim.

After several months of aggressive cold calling and limited success, I unearthed the mother lode, a small 80-person company that was ripe for a benefits change. I spent hours developing my relationship with the decision maker, holding his hand through the various stages of courtship. Lunches, dinners, gifts for his kids. I was doing everything right and all the things I had been taught that could or should influence a decision of this magnitude positively in my favor — running up a healthy expense account in the process. While I was chasing my elephant, my personal insurance practice was dying. I laid everything at the alter of my new prospect. The payday would surely be enough to make my year and to catapult me to the top of the rookie rankings nationwide. All I had hoped for, all at once, would be realized with this one sale.

Then, the unimaginable happened. On the eve of closing my career breaker, the company was sold to a competitor and within several days, my deal was dead — absorbed by the new parent company, leaving me in the cold in favour of the existing business relationships. I was dumbfounded and now broke. My personal insurance business was dead in the water and my landmark deal gone. I was nine months into a rookie business career and already facing ruin, or so I believed at the time.

Over time, I recovered. I slowly rebuilt my personal insurance practice and sprinkled in some solid benefits and pension for good measure. I struck a healthy balance over the next several years that saw me gradually jump the corporate rankings to become among the company's top young performers. My pursuit of the elephant did not produce the fruits I had expected. No big money or high praise came as result. Instead, a valuable lesson on the importance of a balanced approach to business and the management of personal ego that I believe has served me well since.

— Chris Overholt, Florida Panthers

Things which matter most should never be at the mercy of things which matter least.

— *Anonymous*

TOOL TIME

In order to prepare yourself for your entrance into the rat race, you will need the proper tools to keep you organized. Due to the tremendous amount of time, energy and focus placed on time management by corporate America, there has been a flood of accessible and effective tools (seminars, books, and tapes, training sessions) into the marketplace. While advances in technology have made us more efficient, they have also pushed the pace of business to a warp speed, increasing the need for effective time management. Fortunately, technology has also been used to develop tools to help organize, prioritize and maximize your time.

TIME MANAGEMENT SYSTEM

The first purchase (if you have not already pulled the trigger) should be a Franklin Planner© or similar time management system. Franklin Planner© is widely regarded as the best system and is the current industry leader. To order a planner from Franklin Covey, call 1.800.360.8118. (No, cynic, there is no prior or contemplated relationship between Franklin and the Authors — nor between them and any other vendor mentioned herein.)

When purchasing a Franklin Planner© it is important to order the entire program, which includes an instructional tape to help you maximize the usage of the planner. The planner will keep you organized by housing the important information in your personal and professional life. The planner manages your time with the daily calendar pages and acts as a tickler file for things to be remembered weeks, months and years to come. The planner will also provide a place for a daily "To-Do" list and a place to write down the names, numbers and messages from your voice mails, so they will be returned in a timely and professional manner.

This is one aspect of your work life where it is nearly impossible to be too "over the top." Get into the planner and use it to keep you on track. Carry the planner with you to staff meetings, your review, the bank, movies, company retreat, etc. If used properly, the planner will send you on your way to an organized and prioritized career.

Palm Pilot© Your Way Through The Next Century

Technology is playing a large role in taking these planners to the next level. The Palm Pilot© by 3Com is a hand-held computer that allows the user to access a calendar and directory and download information back and forth with your personal computer. The Palm Pilot©, which fits in your shirt pocket, recognizes handwriting and processes the information into the hand held unit. Palm Pilots© have the Franklin Planner© software already installed, making the transition to and use of the units much more user-friendly than anything on the market. Advanced users may also receive and send e-mail from the remote units.

Palm Pilots© are available at Staples© and most other places personal computers are sold. This is the way the world is going. The quicker you can get yourself comfortable and up to speed with the technology, the better off you will be.

ACT!©, Access©

ACT!©, Access©, and Goldmine© are top quality database management systems readily available in the marketplace. These databases are transferable to the Palm Pilot©. These databases store client, supplier, prospect, internal customer and personal information in an easy-to-use-and-access format. The person's name, phone number, address, birthday, spouse's name and any other information they feel is pertinent can be stored and easily retrieved with these systems. The programs also act as a reminder, complete with alarm clock ding for appointments, calls that need to be made at a certain time or birthday cards that need to be sent. The report writing capabilities will allow you to sort your database for your best use.

These programs act as personal assistants. It is essential to show up at meetings on time, follow up when you say you are going to follow up, and keep a realistic schedule that doesn't stretch you to the limits of ineffectiveness. These programs are designed to keep you in line and on time.

Information is power. The proper use of these database programs provides you with the perfect memory. Spouse's names, birthdays, alma maters and notes from the last conversation, etc. are just a few of the pertinent tidbits of information that will be at your fingertips during your next contact with the person. People are always flattered when you remember them and make them more than "just another call you had to make." The personal touch will set you apart and on top of the world.

Take time each week to enter your new contacts into the database. To be an effective tool that saves time and reduces additional work, rather than creating it, the program must be updated regularly and accurately. These programs are also excellent stewards to aid in sending personalized letters and notes. The formats are simple to use and provide a professional finish and look.

These programs also act as calendars and can be used effectively if used in conjunction with a Palm Pilot or Franklin Planner. Remember, to optimize use of a planner, it must be with you at all times. It is very difficult and not very practical to carry a laptop everywhere you go, get it out of the bag, boot it up and punch in a scheduled meeting. A Franklin Planner and Palm Pilot are easy and accessible and the right compliment to ACT!

BE BRIEF

It is important to purchase a briefcase for work. If you do not know what kind of briefcase to buy, find out the type of briefcase your boss has and buy a similar one. Carrying a briefcase makes you look more professional coming and going to work as well as out on meetings. Be careful of the trap of making your briefcase a catchall, where everything with no other place to go ends up. The briefcase should serve as another tool to help keep you organized, not a place to hide things without a proper file folder.

There is no magic trick or secret to utilizing and maintaining an effective briefcase. It often depends on your job description, requirements and mobility. However, there are a few constants when it comes to your briefcase that can apply to you:

- *Keep it clean.* Your briefcase is an extension of what you are and you must take care of it. Throw out paper and junk mail that seems to accumulate.

- *What you need is present.* Extra pen, business cards, information on your company, clients in the area. As a manager of nine salespeople, nothing bothered me more than when a salesperson did not have extra forms or the right forms in his or her briefcase.

- *Make a list of what you need for various meetings and keep the list in your planner.* Review the list prior to a meeting.

WARDROBE PLANNING

Where no plan is laid, where the disposal of time is surrendered

> **merely to the chance of incident, chaos will soon reign.**
> — *Victor Hugo*

Plan, plan, plan. Spend some time on Sunday night planning your various ensembles for the coming week. By the time your head hits the pillow on Sunday night, you should know what you are wearing for the next five days. Go the distance, decide on the suit, socks or stockings, shirt, bra, tie, scarf, underwear, and shoes you will be wearing over the course of the week. If you will be short on shirts, you will have to go to the dry cleaner. If you need socks and underwear, do the laundry that night or plan a night when you will have some time during the week. If something needs to be ironed, do it on Sunday. Avoid scrambling and stressing in the morning by preparing on Sunday night. Your wardrobe is a very important part of your professional career and if you do not review it then it will cause unneeded stress in your life. Polish your shoes each Sunday night. This will keep your shoes looking professional and keep the leather from wearing down.

DO NOT LET WHAT HAPPENED TO ME HAPPEN TO YOU:

I was living at home early in my career and had yet to discover the magician known as the dry cleaner. I only had seven dress shirts, five of which I wore. As much as I hate to admit it, Mom was ironing my shirt for me each night. While my parents were on vacation, I awoke on Tuesday to find an empty shirt closet. Uh oh. I had never ironed a shirt in my life and I did not have much time to learn. I ran to the hamper, threw yesterday's shirt into the dryer for 10 minutes and presto, I had a shirt for the day. I doused myself with cologne and off I went to work. I stayed clear of people the entire day and was paranoid that anyone within 20 feet would smell the shirt and see the wrinkles. The humiliation brought a sense of creativity as I located a one-hour dry cleaner 20 minutes from work. I can assure you today that it will never happen to me again.

— Eric J. Hinds

After eight months in Chicago, I was asked by one of the top executives to move to the firm's headquarters on the East Coast and work in his group. I asked when he needed me and he said ASAP, so I told him I'd be there in two days. I packed that night and started the drive. Upon arriving, I was told that we would be hosting a large conference in NYC the next week and that I should meet my boss at the train station for the 6 a.m. train. I was sleeping on someone's couch at the time and didn't hear the alarm until 5:30. Being new to the area and to corporate America, I quickly decided my best course of action was to drive the 20-25 minutes to the train station and meet up as planned. I ran to my car with just my shoes and suit pants on, carrying everything else. Except my tie, belt or socks. Upon arriving in the train parking lot, I used mud-puddle water to mat my bed-head down and headed in. My new boss didn't even notice at first and was sympathetic and brought me to the NYC office to shave, buy a tie, etc. before we moved on to the conference.

— *Jerome Hepplemann, PBHGF Funds*

Do not let this happen to you. Always be prepared. Keep an extra shirt and tie or blouse in the office in case of emergencies. When the "emergency" does come, and it will, be ready. A spilled coffee, grease from a flat tire, toner from the copier or slip at lunch could ruin your day if you are not prepared. Avoid the worry and the added stress.

Desk Management

So now that we have our shoes polished, our shirts dry-cleaned, our briefcase in perfect filing form we are ready to go work. Now what?

I remember my first day at ADP. I didn't know what to expect or what to do. I was escorted over to meet a friendly fast-talking office manager named Linda Miaullo, who sat me down at my desk and went over all my supplies. It seemed easy enough. I had all the basic desk supplies including computer, stapler, tape, pens, note cards and letterhead. I had a beautiful, clean and organized desk, or so I thought. Then my workday began. Within a week I had about six different piles of paper with Post-it© notes all over my work area. I tried on many different occasions to rid myself of all the paper but it seemed that I was always putting piles off that would never reach their destination. The harder I tried the more disorganized I world become. It was frustrating and I didn't know where to turn.

After a few months I could not take it any more. I wasted valuable time reorganizing my desk and looking for information that should have been at my fingertips. I visited the Sultan of Organization, sales executive Rich Litt, to ask his opinion on how he kept himself organized. Rich was widely known throughout the organization as the most organized man in all of ADP. His desk was always immaculate and he always seemed in control. Rich suggested I meet him 7:00 the next morning and he would show me his system. A savior.

— *Eric J. Hinds*

Many of the Sultan's ideas have been incorporated in the next few sections. The idea is to provide you with a system that is proven to work in hopes that you will use the system, customize it to your job and improve it to make it perfect for you.

SINGLE FILE

The first step is to create files based on all your general topics. As you begin to use this system, it will become quickly evident that there are some files that you need to add. Examples of possible files could be:

    a. Training

    b. Recognition letters

    c. Memos Sent

    d. Memos Received

    e. Product

    f. Competition

    h. Staff Meeting

    i. Administration

    j. Night/Weekend Reading

ONE TOUCH MAGIC

Once you have a solid list of the important files in your daily life it then becomes a filing discipline. As your mail and papers come in, follow one simple rule: touch the mail once. If you pick it up and read it, then file it, pass it on, or throw it away. The wastebasket is an organized person's best friend. Your mail and paperwork either go into one of your files or it goes right for the wastebasket. This discipline is crucial to maintaining an orderly desk.

This system also works well with e-mail. As more and more people have access to e-mail, the more messages you will find in your in-box each morning at work. Select some key times during the day — early morning, when you return from lunch and before you leave at night — to open and respond to your e-mail. If you are going to save the e-mail, save it to your hard drive and delete the message from the in-box. Avoid Post-it© notes, they are the friend of the messy. Organize your to-do list in your planner. Do not let the e-mails pile up in your in-box, they will become overwhelming and important e-mails that require a response will be overshadowed and overlooked.

Steve McClatchy, of Alleer Training and Consulting, offers:

> *If You Can't Do It Today, Don't Look At It Today* — *The basic purpose of "to-do" list is to help you remember to follow through on something you committed to or would like to get done. The problem is when you sit down to create a "to-do" list all the "to-dos" that come to mind, regardless of when they have to be done, often appear on one giant list.*
>
> *These giant "to-do" lists often make us feel overwhelmed, frustrated, trapped and less productive rather than more productive. The most basic function of a day planner is to act as a 365-day "to-do" list. Instead of having one giant, hope-you-lose-it-and-never-find-it-again list, you have 365 little manageable ones that keep you in control and keep you productive. Palm Pilots, Outlook and the like also give you this ability but few people take advantage of this simple function.*
>
> *Think of the power of this one skill. Now if you think of something you can't do until next Wednesday you can put it on next Wednesday's "to-do" list and forget about it. When someone says to you, "Let's keep in touch," you can now go out three months and remind yourself to give them a call or send them an article you just read. If you glance at your planning device every day that task will come back to you all by itself. Your mind is now free to think, be creative, focus, concentrate and even enjoy other things.*
>
> *Creating "future to-do lists," as I like to call them, is the key to long-range goal achievement, effective delegation, project management and one of the most important business skills you can ever develop — contact management. Master this one-time management skill and you will save lots of time as well as significantly improve your ability to be successful.*

Starting the Day on the Right Foot

The first thing to do in the morning is review your schedule for the upcoming day and week to make sure you can accomplish your necessary scheduled tasks and attend all the meetings on your schedule.

Develop a routine each morning. A recommended start is as follows:

- Confirm the day's appointments.

- Return calls of people who left messages overnight or to those whom you did not call back the day before.

- Go through the day file and prioritize the day's activities and block time out to accomplish them in your planner.

- Review your daily calendar and decide what preparation has to be done for upcoming meetings.

- Write the "to-do" list for the day.

Night Time is the Right Time

The organized person ... makes the most of his time and goes to his bed perfectly relaxed for rest and renewal.
— *George Matthew Adams*

There is a tendency to rush out of the office at the end of the day. Take a deep breathe, recap the day, and review the following day's schedule and make sure you are really ready to go home. Before you head home for the night, there are a few things you need to do:

- Review your calendar for the following day and for the coming week. You may have to come in early the next day or go right to an appointment. If you need anything first thing in the morning, make sure you are set to go.

- Check your planner; making sure you have returned all your calls that came in that day.

- Go through your to-do list and make sure all of your urgent items for the day are completed.

- Review your e-mail for the last time.

- Turn off the office lights and set the alarm.

To Do or Not To Do, That is the Question

As you begin to meet and exceed levels of expectation set at work, you will most likely be given increased responsibility and autonomy. Sounds great at first glance, but multiple tasks can be frustrating and debilitating. Without a proper system of classifying your projects, your in-box will continue to pile up and you will accomplish less and less work. It is best to use a grading system for projects that you are assigned. This system should be used to mark tasks in your planner, as well as with your One Touch filing method. Letter grades are easily recognizable:

A — *Always Do Today*. This is the urgent list and should be completed at some point during the day.

B — *Be Prepared to Act*. This is the important list. It is secondary to the A list in order of urgency.

C — *Could Do*. The C list is not a priority and is less important than the B list. If time permits this is the list to take care of. Often times, items on this list can be taken care of later in the week.

D — *Don't Lose Sleep Over This One*. The D list is the icing on the cake. If you get to this list you are really cooking. Often times this list is contained with items that will get you over the top.

More organized and effective prioritizing leads to a fewer number of items that will end up in the A pile. The list should be reviewed each day. Tasks not taken care of should be moved to the following day. When a project is accomplished, check it off your list. The database program ACT! automatically moves unfinished tasks to the next day.

The equalizing force in a day is time. Fortunately, we are all given the same amount. What you accomplish during this time will distinguish you in your career. Working hard allows you to keep your job. Working smart gets you promoted. Having a prioritization system and being organized will help you to get more done with greater efficiency.

Steve McClatchy is the president of Alleer Training & Consulting, a world-class organization that provides training and speaking services in the areas of time management, leadership and sales. Steve has worked in sales, sales management,

Chapter 5

Scoring Goals

The reason most people never reach their goals is that they don't define them, or ever seriously consider them as believable or achievable. Winners can tell you where they are going, what they plan to do along the way, and who will be sharing the adventure with them.
                                                              — Dennis Watley

W e know what you are thinking: You are sick and tired of being lectured about setting goals. You are probably even contemplating skipping this chapter altogether. Don't do it. There is a reason so much is written, spoken, lectured and instructed about goals and the importance of goal setting. It is essential to your career.

An aim in life is the only fortune worth finding.
— *Jacqueline Kennedy Onassis*

training and consulting for such organizations as the Pillsbury Company, Broderbund Software, Franklin Covey and Forte Systems. Alleer's client list includes Major League baseball, NBA, State Farm Insurance, American Cancer Society, TV Guide and the NCAA. Steve McClatchy is widely recognized as a thought leader in time management and offers this advice on time management tips:

Become Observant of Yourself and Others. The first step to becoming a good time manager is to observe the ways you are currently spending your time. If you do it write it down. Take notice of where your time goes and where and with whom you spend it. Once you are aware of where your time goes it will be much easier to determine what you should do differently. The second step is to make better choices. It takes a lot of character to try something new but if you don't change what you're doing, then you'll keep getting exactly what you're getting.

Learn To Say "No." Saying "no" for some people is a very hard thing to do but it has tremendous rewards. Ask yourself, "What is the wisest and best use of my time right now?" If any given opportunity does not meet that criterion, say "no" to the opportunity.

Plan 10 Minutes Every Day. Taking less than 1% of your day to plan the other 99% will yield much more than 10 minutes in return. The many benefits of a written plan include the ability to recover faster from interruptions, to control events instead of events controlling you, to weigh daily opportunities against your plan so you know where your time is best spent and to save the time lost transitioning between tasks. The excuse I hear most often for not planning is, "I don't have time," but really it's time you lose when you don't have a plan.

Prioritize. The Pareto Principle, or the 80/20 rule as it is sometimes called, was discovered by the Italian economist Vilfredo Pareto back in the early 1900s. The Pareto Principle suggests that 80% of the results we get comes from 20% of the things we do. So the question becomes what activities create 80% of the results?

Goals are important and powerful tools in directing your future. It is the commitment and attention to goal setting, follow through and evaluation that will help guide you along the path of success. Successful business people never rest on their laurels, nor congratulate themselves after achieving a goal. Successful people evaluate the process of achievement then set new goals to reach higher. Goals will serve you well if you view life not as a mountain that must be conquered, but as an endless mountain range with different sizes, shapes and heights to climb.

It is always difficult to balance short-term and long-term goals. It is easy early on in your career to focus too much energy on the immediate short term. This is dangerous, as often times people forget to set longer-term goals, which help guide you through tough decisions. There is no doubt you will be faced with these decisions throughout your career. The key is balance. Too much focus on the long term will reduce the effectiveness of short-term action and successes. Remember to have goals set daily, weekly, monthly, and annually and three- to five-year goals. Continually update the goals to stay current and consistent with the times to keep you focused and prepared.

GOAL CHARACTERISTICS

> **The tragedy of life does not lie in not reaching your goal.**
> **The tragedy lies in having no goal to reach.**
> — *Benjamin Mays*

There are universal characteristics to effective goal setting and achieving. If you are going to spend the time, effort and energy to go through the process, make sure you do it right. Before you start, it is important to recognize the characteristics that will help you formulate the structure of the goals you set.

Spell it Out

Goals must be specific. Be as descriptive as you possibly can when setting your goals. It is the difference between shooting in the dark or shooting in the light. Shooting for goals is more attainable if you know exactly what you are shooting for.

Example of an ineffective goal: "I want to be rich."

A more specific goal would be "I want to be a millionaire."

As you will see in the coming sections, even "I want to be a millionaire" is not an effective goal. However, it is more specific and therefore more effective than "I want to be rich." After an initial round of setting goals, remember to ask yourself the question, "Is there a way I can make this goal more specific while maintaining the purpose and intent of the goal?"

Success Point

Effective goals must be measurable. Effective goals have a measurable, objective success point at which it is apparent whether the goal has been achieved. Without a success point, the objective evaluation and self-reflection gets considerably cloudy.

Using the previous example of a specific goal, "I want to be a millionaire," it is clear that although it is specific, there is no success point.

A more effective goal that includes a success point would be: "I want $1,000,000 in assets." There is still room for considerable improvement in this goal, but it is a step in the right direction.

> *I never worked for anyone in my life. So, as my friends headed off to college and I into the work world, I knew it was time to start realizing some of those goals I had hanging on my bedroom door for the last few years. I wanted to be recognized as one of the best remodelers of homes in the country. I was young and looked young. To succeed I would have to be better than everyone else — the quality of work, the level of service and the follow-up all had to be top shelf. That is the path I followed and success continued to bring more work and bigger projects. Recently, I was recognized as one of the "Top 50 remodelers" in the country by "The Journal of Light Construction." I now knew I had to raise the bar.*
>
> *— Tim Cross, Merrick Construction*

Time Will Tell

Effective goals must be time constrained. The goal setter should set a period for when the goal will be achieved. This is another important step in helping you to evaluate your progress toward the success point.

Improving on the aforementioned goal by making it timely is quite simple: "$1,000,000 in assets by the time I turn 30 years old." Now we are getting somewhere. This goal is timely, has a success point and is specific. Unless you are very fortunate, this is also a stretch goal, which is the topic to be discussed in the next section.

Reach for the Sky

> **Aim at heaven and you get earth thrown in;**
> **aim at earth and you get neither.**
> — *C. S. Lewis*

Most conventional goal setting books, seminars and teachings will tell you to be realistic when setting goals. The thought process, though misguided, is simple: Goals that are too lofty often times result in failure. Was Fred Smith realistic when he started FedEx and took on the U.S. Postal Service? Was Bill Gates realistic when he took on Big Blue? How could we ever progress as a nation if we had settled for realistic goals? Inventions are discovered, companies are made and individuals reach to new heights when, and only when, they push themselves to reach beyond what seems obtainable.

Ever since high school I had wanted to get my MBA from Harvard Business School. This might seem realistic for some blue bloods who have spent their youths bouncing from prep school to the agonizing decision of which Ivy League school to attend to Wall Street or consulting then back to business school and probably at Harvard (or Stanford or Wharton). Well, that just was not me. I did not exactly make history with my SAT score and subsequently was turned down from all but two of the nine undergraduate universities to which I had applied.

Harvard Business School strongly recommends at least three years of work experience before applying to the business school. The more I researched the process, the slimmer my chances seemed. The class traditionally took 113 of its incoming students from investment banking and 113 from consulting. My sports marketing job was not looking like a slam-dunk of any sorts. The shot of me getting into HBS was so slim, I was too embarrassed to tell anyone but my wife that I was applying.

But this was a goal I had carried since high school and I was determined to give it my best shot. I wrote and re-wrote the best essays, got the best recommendations and delivered in the interview, which gave me the best chance of success. Never stop trying and pushing.

— *Scott M. O'Neil*

Scott was accepted into the Harvard Business School Class of 1998 and would be selected by his classmates to deliver the commencement address at graduation.

Only after you continually shoot for the stars, will you ever have the chance to realize your true potential. Think about this concept for a few minutes. There is tremendous inherent risk with this philosophy. With every acceptance to Harvard Business School for Scott, there was the time he was cut from the Villanova basketball team. Scott was wait-listed and later rejected from Notre Dame. He received rejection letter after rejection letter in his torturous job search after college. All of that rejection hurts, but they became the chips on his shoulders that would drive him to succeed. Don't you want to know how high you can fly?

I had always relished the role of the underdog. I think that is why I chose Villanova, because it had built the reputation as the prototypical underdog school. What a match? After making the team as a non-scholarship walk-on player my first two years, the soccer coach told me there was a 90% chance that I would not make the team the following year. That summer I worked out harder than I ever thought possible. I returned to school the next year and not only made the team, but also earned a starting position. Over the next two years, I would be named Big East Player of the Week two times and co-captain of the team.

— *Eric J. Hinds*

Goals are set to get you to a higher ground and test your limits. It is okay to fail. If you are shooting 100% you are selling yourself short and inhibiting your growth. You must learn and gain strength each time you slip and fall. Only then can you appreciate the true exhilaration of success.

Too many times we are sucked into thinking there are limits to what we can achieve. These are boxes, bubbles, and restraints we put on ourselves, or worse yet, we let others put them on and around us. Is it your parents, siblings, friends, coaches, classmates, boss who put this ring around your potential? Actually, it is you. This is where you have control and you should use it. If you look at the very successful people in the world, many of them broke through the barriers and constraints to achieve goals and greatness.

> *As a first-year sales rep at ADP, the execs would hammer the rookies to set realistic goals. They would actually deter first-year people from setting a goal of reaching President's Club. "No one had ever done it before. It was unrealistic," they said. "Just concentrate on a hitting plan and you will be fine," they continued. Little did they know, they had already set my goal. That year I vacationed in Vail with the rest of the President's Club winners.*

> — Eric J. Hinds

Remember to aim for the stars, but understand that you are shooting high, because, if you only hit the moon you are a lot further along then you would have been otherwise.

Try this exercise to further demonstrate stretch goals: Stand up against the wall and reach high to the ceiling with both arms. Now reach higher. Again reach higher. For the last time reach still higher. This time we are serious: reach higher again. The last reach, when you think it is out of the realm of possibility to go any higher and you manage to go up another inch, represents a "stretch goal," hence the name.

Apply this type of thinking when setting your goals. This is the only way to push yourself and begin to approach your potential. Scott has had and continues to develop a number of stretch goals throughout his life. Early on in his life he reached for the stars. Making the freshman basketball team as an eighth-grader and being elected class president of his high school when he started his first day only knowing one person (his brother) were realized goals during his formative years. He later sought to become the youngest vice president in NFL history, which he accomplished at the ripe old age of 28. There are also a number of current stretch goals out there now: writing a book. He always had the perception that he was not a good writer (so he became a writer and editor of the Harvard Business School newspaper and decided to write a book). Scott would also like to become the president of a major league sports team before he turns 36 years old.

PERSONAL VS. PROFESSIONAL

> *I started at my company about 7 1/2 years ago in a class of six other guys. One was a tax attorney, one guy a Harvard grad, one guy a former Villanova football player, and a couple other guys who were my age and also seemed to be infinitely more qualified to succeed at my business than I felt I was. My goal when I started this career was to make it just that, a career,*

and not just another "stepping stone" job where I'd have to update my resume in a couple of years. I picked my industry because it provided a lot of things I was looking for: unlimited income potential, schedule flexibility (after the initial couple of years), ability to meet a lot of people, and not having to sit in front of a computer all day. 7 1/2 years after starting, there's only one other guy who I started with still in the business. Not that I'm a "success," but I feel like I was successful at keeping in mind that I started at this company and in this industry because of what the long-term rewards would be. My income isn't stifled and is based solely on how hard, and more importantly, how smart I work. My schedule, therefore, becomes more flexible and will allow me to do things down the road like play Wiffle ball with my kids (when I have some) every night, just like my dad did when I was growing up.

Some of my closest friends now are people I've met simply because of what I do for a living, and I'm rarely in the office all day, except when I need to stay in and do planning. I'm no overnight success, or even a true success at this point, but the reason I'm still here is because I was able to handle what seems like a million emotional and financial failures or problems over the past 7 1/2 years — and succeed at staying focused on why I picked this industry and this company when I first started.

— Michael Root, Creative Financial Group

Remember to balance goals between personal and professional. The inclination as a young, rising wanna-be professional is to focus all of your time and energy developing your professional goals. It is easy to fall into this trap of challenging yourself in one area and neglecting another. Both personal and professional goal setting are essential to your development and future success. Professional goals are work- and career-related. Personal goals are the wide range of other goals ranging from personal development, educational, spiritual, health, family, etc. The more you develop personally, the quicker your career goals will be realized. When you feel good about yourself personally and are accomplishing your personal goals, you will be more apt to be able to reach your professional goals.

To stay or not to stay — that is the tough question most people face early on in their careers. For me, it was the toughest professional decision I had faced. I had been with the same company for five years and kept looking for a senior person in the company I could model myself after, both personally and professionally.

Jim Maltese at Merrill Lynch seemed to do it right: He was a great father, my soccer coach growing up, involved in his church and very successful professionally. He has found the right balance and was the same guy helping to recruit me to my current employer. Jim still says today that the more attention he gives to his personal life, the more effective he is at work.

— Eric J. Hinds

This is the hardest thing to realize as a young professional. It is difficult to relate the importance of your relationships with your parents, siblings, girlfriend, and friends to your success at work. If you live the life of the young successful tiger at work, you must bring that energy and enthusiasm to your personal life as well.

Steps To Success

Goal setting is a discipline that can be learned. There is a structure and process you must follow for setting and achieving effective goals. The following is an effective and proven step-by-step process for setting goals:

Some advice I got early in my career from the past president of Sanford (Paul Donahue) was not to get caught up in thinking about your next promotion or assignment because then you would lose focus on your daily tasks and responsibilities. It is wonderful to have personal goals and objectives, but don't let them take over what you should be doing on an everyday basis.

His quote to me that I will never to this day forget was, "Do the best job in the role that you are currently in. People in the organization will notice the solid job that you are doing and they will get you to where you need to be in the organization."

This has been an important piece of advice that I have passed along to the people I manage.

— Brad Brusa, Sanford Corp

Step 1: Get Started

When you determined what you want, you made the most important decision in your life. You have to know what you want in order to attain it.
— Douglas Lurtan

The most difficult thing for a non-goal setter is getting started. Fortunately it is up to you. You can do it. It doesn't cost anything and the risk reward benefits can be tremendous. If you are having trouble, start with a couple of small, attainable goals. Living without goals is like trying to sail a ship without a rudder. The time is now to get your mindset ready to begin the process.

Step 2: Visualize the End Result

Before a painter puts a brush to his canvas he sees his picture mentally. If you think of yourself in terms of a painting, what do you see? Is the picture one you think worth painting? You create yourself in the image you hold in your mind.
— Thomas Dreier

There must be a vision of the end result. Visualize how the end of achieving the goal feels, sounds and tastes. The more clear the vision of the end, the more effective you will be in following through on your actionable steps. This is often times difficult and routinely skipped by amateur goal setters.

As a young man, I got my first job as a grunt with a small company on the American Stock Exchange. I knew my first day on the job that I had found my career and knew shortly thereafter that this was the company I wanted to run some day. Maybe I was too young and naive to know how unrealistic this was at the time, which was probably the best thing for me.

As time went on I received one promotion to the next. I continued to work long hours — the first few years in the financial industry are very tough on young people — and began to build my reputation in the industry. Many times I was offered jobs paying more money with bigger titles, but my dream was to run the company where I started. As time would pass I eventually became CEO and owner of one of the largest specialists firms on the exchange.

— Jack Stokes

**Jack Stokes would later sell his company near the top in March of 2001.

Step 3: Write the Goals Down on Paper

A goal is a dream with a deadline.
— Harvey Mackay

A goal is merely a dream until it is written down on paper or typed into a computer. The act of writing and/or typing acts to reinforce the message in your subconscious. It also acts as a constant reminder that the goal is real and something you want to accomplish.

Step 4: Consider the Goal Characteristics Above

Throughout the goal setting and achieving process, continue to review the aforementioned goal characteristics. Staying within the parameters set will keep you on the right path and focused.

Step 5: Hang Goals in Multiple Places

Select one or two most important goals and tape them on your bathroom mirror, on your refrigerator, on your phone, in your car and on your desk at work. The more you are reminded of the goal the deeper the imprint the goal will make on your subconscious and direct your thoughts of completing the goal to the conscious. You need to be constantly reminded, which will strengthen your will and direct your decisions.

Step 6: Set Action Plan

Did you ever wonder why New Year's resolutions rarely are completed and accomplished? Normally, it is because the resolutions are written at the height of holiday time and sealed in an envelope never to be heard of again until 12 months later. The key to achieving goals is to set an action plan to complete. Sit down and write it out. Decide how you are going to get there. Sketch out a time line with completion dates. Most goals you set will not be able to be accomplished in one sitting and a written action plan is the only way to get you on your way.

Step 7: Commit to Making the Right Decisions

> **You can't push a person up a ladder unless he wants to climb.**
> — *Andrew Carnegie*

Commit to making the right decisions and accomplishing these goals. This sounds simple, but this is one of the toughest parts of the equation. Achieving your goals, especially if they are stretch goals, is not easy and you will have to sacrifice. The sacrifice might mean cutting out aimless television watching or a second helping, or waking up at 5:00 each morning to get an extra hour of planning, but it will cost you somewhere. It is necessary to understand you must be willing, committed and capable to be successful.

Step 8: Set Periodic Evaluation Times and Check-ups

The only way to continue to progress toward your goal is to set periodic checks to evaluate your progress. Goals must have intermittent success points to evaluate how you are doing in your process. Find out where you stand in the overall goal process and make necessary adjustments to assure you are on the path to achieving the success point.

Step 9: Reward Yourself for Achieving — and Evaluate Misses

This is the fun part, especially if you are on course and hitting your targets and equaling or exceeding your timeline. A good friend had set his own sales goal each year. For each milestone he would hit along the way, he would buy himself a Hugo Boss tie. Not exactly my idea of a celebration, but it was his. Take yourself to a ball game or splurge on new clothes. However, beware of the trap. For example, if your goal is to lose weight do not reward yourself with Big Mac and a hot fudge sundae. Also, if your goal is to pay off your credit card debt before the end of the year, charging a five-star dinner is probably not the answer either.

It is equally important to evaluate misses as it is to reward successes. Find out why you are not on target. Ask yourself if you are doing everything you can to achieve the goal. Are you living up to the commitments you set forth? Is the action plan aggressive enough to reach your goal? If not, make the necessary adjustments to get yourself back on course. If achieving the goal is important enough, you will find a way. You might have to readjust and alter your action plan. Don't allow yourself to stay on the current course or you will fall short.

Step 10: Raise the Bar

Make no small plans. They'll never have the power to move men's souls.
— *P.T. Barnum*

Continue to set and evolve goals and raise the bar when you begin to reach and exceed the goal set forth. When Scott first got to Villanova, he set a goal to get a grade point average of 3.0. He exceeded this his first semester without knowing the system, so he raised the bar to wanting to graduate with honors (3.5), which he managed to achieve. What if the goal had been summa cum laude or even magna cum laude? You never know unless you reach for it. Another example is when Scott had finally achieved his lifelong goal of getting accepted to the Harvard Business School and arrived on the Harvard campus determined to make a lot of friends and a difference. Scott raised the bar again. He was elected by his classmates to deliver the graduation speech to more than 8,000 people who assembled to celebrate the weekend.

Chapter 6

Giving, Receiving and Enjoying Feedback

No matter how much a man can do, no matter how engaging his personality may be, he will not advance far in business if he can't work through others.

— *John Craig*

Josh Weston, CEO of ADP, often used a pertinent example to clearly send a message that he expected the bar to continually be raised. As the leading payroll services provider in the world and leader of a company that still holds the record for most consecutive quarters of double-digit growth, Weston urges people not to be satisfied with "just" being number one. He would cite the plight of the Olympic pole-vaulter. Even after the pole-vaulter has won the gold and been crowned the best in the world, the athlete continues to raise the bar until the bar is knocked down three times. Even when one is the best, the person is asked to push to the absolute limits and raise the bar as high as they can go. Are you willing to go to these lengths and test yourself?

The great thing about goals is they are yours. They can be as public or private as you want them to be. Following the process above will help lead you down the right hallway to the right doors. Goals are not etched in stone. People change, as do goals that people set. A goal you set five years ago might not apply to you now, but as long as it is relevant it will lead you to the door and it is then your choice to accept and open the door, or set other goals and move on to something else.

T his chapter focuses on the importance of feedback in the workplace. Feedback soothes the natural thirst of wanting to know how others see us. The first part concentrates on steps to take in order to elicit feedback from others. The second part provides a step-by-step process to help you deliver quality feedback. It is not easy and it takes time to develop, but it is very rewarding.

Do you really know how you are doing at work? Should you wait until your annual review to find out? Do you give credit where credit is due? What is the best way to recognize others? Learning how to communicate effectively in the workplace will dramatically and positively alter the path of your career. The essential ingredient to effective communication is feedback — giving, receiving and enjoying.

What is Feedback?

Feedback is the art of providing constructive, objective and unemotional replay of one's actions, words or deeds in the effort to provide the receiver with a better understanding of the impact of the actions. Any feedback is better than no feedback at all.

Receiving timely, accurate and effective feedback is essential to succeeding in your career. Unfortunately there will be tremendous challenges to overcome in order to receive this feedback. Most people are not schooled in the art of giving, receiving or enjoying feedback. Your boss will probably not give you feedback unless you take proactive steps to make it happen. Some bosses are so uncomfortable giving negative feedback to employees they would rather just internalize the frustration or, worse yet, spread the negative feelings to other employees. Others are not properly trained in providing effective feedback. Still other bosses opt to save feedback for formalized settings, which unfortunately are usually semi-annual at best.

Start with your Friends

It is your first day on the job and the president of the company assembles everyone in the cafeteria to announce some new initiatives the management will implement over the coming months. This is probably not the time to chase the president down in the hallway and offer your "feedback." Give yourself time to get acclimated first. Learn how things work and who you can approach. Then start slowly. Begin to give your friends outside of work feedback first and get some practice in. As with most things, you will get better with practice.

When you get comfortable enough, start giving feedback to friends and peers at work. This is a whole other experience to work with. Be very careful offering feedback to your boss. Nine times out of 10 it is a bad idea, a very bad idea. Unfortunately, most of your bosses will probably not be the type of person looking for feedback. A mishap in this area might result in a negative feeling toward you — you might be passed over for a promotion, generate a bad review or even lose your job. This risk/reward ratio is not in your favor, unless of course the feedback is positive.

MISCONCEPTION? WHAT MISCONCEPTION?

There is a widespread misconception among most people that feedback should be negative. The widespread thought is that feedback should always be to help you improve, correct a mistake or change a behavior. This is not the case! Feedback should be about 50/50 positive/negative. If it is lopsided one way or the other, it is a good indication that you need to evaluate both the feedback provider's and the feedback receiver's (your) actions.

> *I had been so nervous all day in the office about this presentation I had to give it had ruined my entire day. Who could blame me? It was my first presentation in front of the entire staff at ADP Princeton. I started a little rocky, but finished strong and was happy with the overall talk. As I was heading back to my desk, the division vice president actively tracked me down and asked if I wanted some feedback. I got defensive and barely heard a word he was saying. He was very complimentary and I kept waiting to hear the word "but" that would highlight what he wanted me to change. I was pleasantly surprised to find how the DVP continued to provide specific examples how I had made a positive impact on the sales force. It was my first introduction to positive feedback and it is a lesson I will never forget. I smiled the whole way home.*
>
> — Eric J. Hinds

IS FEEDBACK REALLY IMPORTANT?

> **What is the shortest word in the English language that contains the letters a, b, c, d, e and f? Answer: Feedback. Don't forget that feedback is one of the essential elements of good communication.**
> — Anonymous

Why spend time on feedback? It is not something you can control, or is it? Actually, yes! You can direct and control the flow of feedback. There is more at stake than your personal development, as feedback tempers the ebb and flow of communication. The need for feedback revolves around human nature. People are more effective when and if they know good versus bad, effective versus ineffective and the difference between positive versus negative behavior and how these actions are valued in the organization.

A common response in exit interviews of 20-somethings when asked why they are leaving the company is lack of feedback received. It is said in many different forms and perceived many different ways. Some samples include:

"I just did not feel comfortable. It was like I did not know what they wanted."

"I wish I knew how my boss felt about me before I said I was leaving. It took my resignation to know I had been doing great. He acted as if he was losing his son when I told him. Yet, I had not really spoken to him in three weeks."

"I thought I was doing great until my review. It hit me like a ton of bricks and that is when I started looking. I want to be successful. How can I get better if I don't know what I am doing wrong?"

"My boss exploded on me after I made the smallest mistake."

"I wish I knew how I could be better. I just don't know what was expected of me."

"I don't like to be complimented all the time by my boss. It feels like she is humoring me. I know when I make a mistake and I am okay with some criticism, but it is awkward, almost as if she avoids me."

Everyone needs to know how he or she is doing and what needs improvement. Is your boss the one to blame? Partly, but as you point one finger at your boss, your four other fingers are pointing right back at yourself. You have a responsibility to be proactive in seeking out feedback.

FEEDBACK IS ONLY BAD WITH STEREO SPEAKERS

The key is to place your emphasis on performance-enhancing feedback. Once accepted and understood in the workplace, take the concept and model of feedback into your personal and family life. Feedback will greatly improve your relationships with your parents, siblings and friends. Most of the emphasis in this chapter will be focused on how to seek out, accept and react to performance enhancing feedback.

Feedback is important for a number of reasons:

1. *Provides information*. It is tremendously beneficial to have accurate and current information about yourself and the impact you have on others. Imagine if you could read people's minds after you interacted with them. You would know when you upset them, made them smile, happy, upset, etc. Feedback is the key to the door.

2. *Self-perceptions are rarely accurate*. For example, you might think you are a funny person and enjoy telling a joke now and again. Unfortunately, the jokes may be inappropriate or put people down. Unless you receive feedback letting you know that the jokes are inappropriate, how would you ever know? We all have a picture of ourselves and how other people see us, which is not necessarily accurate. Feedback will give you a better understanding of how you and your accompanying actions are perceived.

3. *The door is ajar*. Feedback allows you the opportunity to demonstrate that your lines of communication are open. Send the message that you are flexible and willing to adapt, which will give a boss more confidence that you have the capacity to change. The world of business is changing fast. Companies are looking for people who are able to react positively to change. By initiating and responding positively (not defensively) to feedback, it sends a message that you want to improve and are looking to work to make yourself more of an asset to the organization.

4. *Inexperience is prevalent*. Most supervisors you will have in your first or second job will not have had experience in giving feedback. Others are not comfortable confronting people and are not sure how to do it effectively. Both giving and receiving feedback will prepare you for an eventual position in management, where feedback will become your lifeline with your employees, customers, suppliers, bosses, etc. As a young up-and-coming star, you can provide people with whom you interact an example of how to deliver feedback.

5. *Competitive advantage*. Few peers will have exposure to feedback, providing you with an added advantage to advance. Being schooled in the proper art of feedback will set you apart from the pack.

6. *Home improvement*. Feedback will provide specific information about what you did or did not do well. If you are open to continuous improvement and want to be successful, feedback will provide you an avenue of growth and development. This is a tremendous advantage over your peers. Feedback will provide you a blueprint of how to succeed.

7. *Road map.* Feedback provides a better indication of what the boss values. For example, your boss could place higher values on flexibility, leadership, task orientation, etc . The more you understand where your boss places emphasis, the easier it is to prioritize and place your emphasis in those areas. Feedback is also the road map of success, leading you to place emphasis in the right place.

8. *Snapshot.* Feedback provides a clear picture of your actions at a specific point in time. It is almost as if a Polaroid snapshot has been taken. If given properly, feedback should capture you at a moment in time.

Walking the Steps to Quality Feedback

The ball is in your court. You cannot count on everyone else to set the tone for effective feedback in the workplace. It is up to you to be proactive in an effort to get the feedback ball rolling. Nine out of 10 frontline managers will not provide effective feedback. Knowing your boss might not provide timely, accurate and effective feedback, the following are steps to get you started and effectively handle feedback:

Step 1: Remember It Is About You

Never lose sight of the fact that this feedback is for you. Not only will it point to ideas of emphasis on which to focus, it will also improve your relationships. Whether positive or negative, accept the feedback for what it is: someone's perception of your actions. This is your career and feedback is a tool to hasten your development and advancement.

Step 2: Listen Actively

> **Are you really listening or are you just waiting for your turn to talk?**
> —R. Montgomery

In my first year out of college, I was out to save the juvenile delinquents of the world. I worked for a non-profit company that housed adolescents recently found guilty of non-violent crimes. The kids stayed in a house with plenty of staff (like me), and were subject to a rigid daily school and chores schedule, along with very light security. I was convinced that my boss, a man with some 15 years experience in the business, was dead wrong in his approach to dealing with the residents. He strongly advocated for strict adherence to rules, and lectured the staff long and hard against befriending the residents. I, being the young idealist that I was, held a nearly opposite view — that these kids had had a lifetime of poor interpersonal relationships, and that all they really needed was a quality peer relationship (i.e., friendship) with a responsible, educated young adult. I was therefore typically, albeit (noting my boss's presence) soft, on the enforcement of house rules.

One night, just as the youths were headed to bed, and after we had just completed a fun-filled game of pool, one particularly troubled kid, toward whom I had directed a great deal of my friendly efforts, came to me and warmly shook my hand. I was elated. This was evidence that my approach "worked." Fifteen minutes later, during a routine "bed check" the very kid who had shaken my hand moments before (along with his roommate) was missing, and as I looked disbelievingly around the room, I observed a bed sheet tied to the bunk leading out the window. In shaking my hand, the kid who I thought I had such an impact on was not thanking me but saying good-bye, thus fully taking advantage of my naivete.

Thankfully, the youths were shortly thereafter apprehended. But this was an eye-opening experience for me. I still did not necessarily agree that the boss had it all right, but realized that much could be learned from his experience.

— *Sean O'Neil, Gibson Dunn*

Despite your innermost thoughts, you don't know it all. This is not the time to humor anyone. Listen to what is being said and internalize it. If you need further clarification on the information offered, ask follow-up questions. As you listen, also look for the message being conveyed.

STEP 3: TEST FOR UNDERSTANDING

How well we communicate is determined not by how well we say things, but by how well we are understood.
— *Andrew Grove*

This is probably not a phrase you are familiar with, but it is the only way to assure yourself and the feedback provider that you understand the message. Restate information in your own words to clarify and to be certain you have heard feedback and understood it correctly. Ask feedback providers if this is how they intended it.

STEP 4: HELP SENDER

Sometimes the sender of the feedback is uncomfortable delivering the message. Your esponse, body language, and tone of voice can help the sender take more risks and provide more timely and effective feedback. It is never easy to hear what you did wrong or could improve on, and it is just as difficult for others to hear what they did right. However, if you want to be more effective, this is the path. Be a good receiver.

Take the Bull by the Horns

Unless you are working in a high quality corporate environment that pours training hours and big dollars into the lower management levels of the organization, you will probably have to initiate and then sculpt the feedback you receive from your boss, peers or associates. Ask for feedback. Does this sound simple? It depends on who your supervisor, peers or associates are, but the key is to ask. The following example describes a potential approach you might take.

> You: Nancy, if you have a minute, I would like to ask for your help.
>
> Nancy (boss):   Sure, come on in.
>
> You: Could you give me some feedback on the presentation we made to IBM this morning?

This is the first step in initiating feedback, but you still have a long way to go. Your boss, who is probably very busy, will probably respond in one of the following ways:

Great! Good job. Or, I thought it went well.

Unfortunately, these comments do not get you any closer to that corner office. Nancy's response has not helped you at all, except maybe for a short-term ego boost. This is the feedback moment of truth. This is where you need to use your skills to take it a step further. The following are some key phrases and characteristics on which to focus your energy when taking feedback from the "great" message to an effective level.

Get Specific

It is important that the feedback you receive is specific rather than general. "Great" is general. You must ask the provider to get more detailed by furthering the questions and asking for more specifics. Follow up the "great" response with the question: Could you be more specific about what was great about it? Then it is your turn to stop and listen. Continue to ask second and third level questions to follow up until you have received specific information.

FOR EXAMPLE

Examples are an excellent way to get better insight into what the sender of feedback i actually sending through to the message and crystallize the thoughts. Simply ask:

Could you give me an example of this?

EFFECTS

Often times, this is implicit, but other times further clarification is necessary anc prudent. This will help the receiver understand the ramification of the actions. This wil play a dual role, helping the receiver and the sender both to consider the far reachin and lasting effects that may result. You might ask:

How does this behavior affect the organization/division/you?

DESCRIPTIVE VERSUS EVALUATIVE

Help the sender provide descriptive feedback as opposed to evaluative feedback Descriptive feedback provides specifics to help the receiver understand the challenge Evaluative feedback attacks the person, not the action. Evaluative feedback is both judgmental and subjective and is more apt to help the sender than the receiver.

DESCRIPTIVE EXAMPLE:

Boss: *Your preparation and concise knowledge of the material was evident in your presentation. You spoke clearly and covered all the information. The effect of your delivery helped the management team understand the project and where you will need future assistance.*

EVALUATIVE EXAMPLE:

Boss: *You did a good job. The presentation was interesting and we all really enjoyed it. It wil give you some extra points come bonus time.*

KAIZEN

Kaizen is the Japanese word for constant improvement. You need to focus you attention and energy, as well as that of the sender, on what you can control. There will be many circumstances beyond your control that will get a majority of the attention. Do not get sucked into that type of thinking. Emphasize that you will do everything in your control to make the right decisions for the organization. An example of a question you may ask is:

am always looking to improve. Is there something I could have done differently to be more effective?

TIMELY

Last, push for timely feedback. If you give a presentation, ask for feedback within 24 hours. The closer the feedback is to the action, the more details the sender will remember.

Remember all bosses, peers, associates, etc. will react differently with the different approaches you take to requesting feedback. Get to know the person you will be approaching and anticipate the various responses the person might have to your request.

STEP 5: ACKNOWLEDGE WHAT YOU HEAR

Let the sender know that you understand the nature of your behavior and will make the effort to correct it in the future. Continually ask the sender to be more specific to help you better understand the message. Ask the sender to use examples of phrases, body language or actions you demonstrated to trigger the feedback. Examples will crystallize the picture of your behavior in your mind and help you to recall your actions at a later time. It is important to understand the effects of your behavior observed by the sender.

STEP 6: THANK THE SENDER

Simple, but important. Everyone appreciates gratitude and thanks. The thank-you can be written, e-mailed or spoken. By thanking the sender, you will be telling the sender that you welcome feedback. You will receive more feedback as a result.

STEP 7: REVIEW YOUR INTENTIONS

Once you have heard and understood the feedback on your behavior and its effects, revisit your intentions. Evaluate your thought process in the decision you made or the action you undertook that prompted the feedback and review the situation. Take some time to write out how you will handle the situation the next time it arises, because it will.

STEP 8: TAKE ACTION OR DON'T TAKE ACTION

Not all feedback will be helpful or positive. After reviewing the entire process, determine to either continue the behavior or change your behavior as appropriate. Remember it is rarely easy to give feedback. Someone thought it was important enough to spend time and energy to provide you with the information. Take the input seriously. Perception is reality; recognize that the perception is real.

GIVING FEEDBACK

The previous section focused on receiving feedback and ensuring that you take the necessary steps to allow a proper flow of constructive information. This section will provide a process to help you deliver feedback to others.

Giving feedback effectively is a tough task. There are three types of feedback you can provide: *upward, lateral* and *downward.* Upward feedback is delivered to a direct boss or anyone higher up on the corporate ladder. Lateral feedback is delivered to your peers or others carrying similar amounts of perceived power in an organization. Downward feedback is delivered to people reporting to you or to those who carry less perceived power.

Upward feedback is particularly difficult to deliver early on in your career. Remember, often times lower level managers might not welcome feedback. They are often saddled with low confidence and a big ego. As a young employee, it is often difficult to communicate in this fashion to your bosses. Lateral feedback is also challenging. Peers often feel patronized (with positive feedback) or insulted (with negative feedback). Although downward feedback might be the easiest of the three to deliver as a young executive, there is still a danger in the delivery. Be careful not to come off as an arrogant, cocky, know-it-all.

> One of the toughest jobs to survive in is a financial consultant (stockbroker). The average success rate hovers around 20% for first-year associates. In other words, 80% of those who start find other careers within 12 months. For women, the industry gets even tougher. This is a male dominated field (nearly 10 men for every one woman) and it can be intimidating and at times even uncomfortable.

> As a young female broker, I was determined to be one of the 20%. I kept getting denied what I thought was my fair share of I.P.O. shares, which are usually doled based on performance. I was frustrated because I was doing great and beating almost everyone in the office in new accounts and volume. I knew if I had complained in such a male dominated office, I was running the risk of being an outcast. So, I went to the managing partner and delivered some feedback that I, along with some of the guys, would love a training that could explain the process of obtaining I.P.O. shares so that it would be more clear and fair for all brokers. I was very specific in my delivery of the feedback about the uncertainty, uneasiness, and unfairness around the allocation.

My feedback changed the office policy. Three weeks later a policy was established and published (within the office). The managing partner was unaware of the uncertainty and the stress it caused and was appreciative of the feedback.

— *Leslie Swift, PaineWebber*

If you are convinced you are ready to provide feedback, it is important that you are very aware of your surroundings, people's feelings and the potential risk/reward scenarios. Delivering effective feedback will strengthen your relationships with those you interact with, as well as prepare you for your future as a supervisor.

STEP 1: DOES THE PERSON WANT TO HEAR IT?

Before you start dishing out the feedback, you first have to ask the potential receiver if he would like feedback. It can be as simple as: "John, are you open to some feedback on the conversation we just had?" If the answer is no, the person is not ready and you might want to approach the subject later on in the day or week. If the answer is yes, you are in business and ready to go.

STEP 2: BE TIMELY

The best-case scenario for dispensing feedback is to deliver it as nearly immediately after the event as possible. This is so the person receiving the feedback will be able to most vividly remember the details of the event. The closer the feedback is to the actual event or happening, the greater the impact. It is necessary to be more descriptive the longer the time lapse.

STEP 3: BE DESCRIPTIVE

Feedback is not the time to play judge, jury and executor. If you find yourself in this role, you are missing the essence of feedback altogether. Do not be judgmental or evaluative. Your objective is to be as descriptive as possible. Remember you are trying to help the person. If it is positive feedback, it will serve as reinforcement for that person to repeat the actions, tone or words. The feedback is intended to let the person know what was positive so that she can repeat the similar actions in the future if the same situation arises. It is helpful to be as descriptive as possible to provide the receiver with a vivid understanding and account of the action.

No Solutions

This is the number one faux paux in delivering feedback. Your advice is not welcome here. This is not a Dear Abby column. Feedback provides details of the event and the effect it had on others.

Step 4: Stay Constructive

It is always tempting to sway to destructive commentary when providing feedback. When the conversation becomes destructive, the receiver will eventually tune you out. You will have lost the opportunity to help the person develop. Constructive feedback is not to be confused with constructive criticism. There is no criticism, constructive or otherwise in this feedback. Feedback is designed with the recipient in mind. Keep this in mind and keep it constructive.

Step. 5: Use Examples

Examples help a person form a clear vision of what was said, how a person feels or what can make the person perform at the highest potential. Reference specific words, cues or actions to help the receiver recall the specifics.

Step 6: Make the Person Aware of the Impact and Effect

In the ebb and flow of business, we often forget that how we act and interact with others affects the lives and feelings of others. Feedback helps as a reminder. The receiver should be made aware of the impact the discussion, words, actions had on others, specifically you. In the effort to make someone aware of her actions through positive feedback, you might talk about her bringing a smile to your face, or the actions that made you feel more comfortable and less threatened. Be specific with the impact. Begin your sentences with: The effect on the group was ... The impact your actions had was ...

Step 7: Be Specific

The more specific you can be both of the actions that led to the feedback and the effect the actions had, the more effective the feedback will have on the receiver. Use the most descriptive and appropriate adjectives to help the person better understand the situation.

Step 8: Test for Understanding

The final step is to test for understanding to assure the receiver has heard you correctly. The best course here is to ask the receiver to reiterate his understanding of the feedback. After you have delivered the meat of the

Chapter 7

Beaming With Confidence

Experience tells you what to do; confidence allows you to do it.
— *Stan Smith*

feedback, test for understanding. For example: I would like to test for understanding. Can you reiterate your understanding of this feedback?

Like French, Spanish or Italian, feedback is a language you must learn to speak. Read, learn and practice the structure we have set forth. Opening lines of communication will help your personal and professional relationships and further your career. Whether a partnership at work or home, the key ingredient to success is effective two-way communication.

P rofessional sports provide myriad stories about overmatched players with heart, determination and character that overcome, reach their goals and succeed. Today's athletes are bigger, faster and stronger than ever before. Their skills are refined and perfected as the most advanced technological machinery is put to use. But there is no machine, computer or drug that can build an athlete's greatest asset — confidence.

How many times did John Elway lead the Denver Broncos in a come-from-behind last minute drive to win the game? Did he have the strongest arm? Fastest legs? Was he the smartest quarterback? The quarterback with the best system? Yet when Elway was in the huddle backed up on his own 10-yard line with 2:00 left on the clock and his team trailing by six points, there was only one thing that mattered. The players in the huddle, the other team's defense, the fans in the stands and those watching at home all knew Elway was going to drive the length of the field and score. You could see it in his eyes, every time the camera focused on a closeup. Everyone was swept away by the magic — his confidence.

There is simply no substitute for confidence. It allows you to maximize your performance in sports and in the work force.

WHAT IS SELF-CONFIDENCE?

Self-confidence is the trust and belief in one's own ability and the feeling of inner strength that creates a certain aura around your personality. Self-confidence helps you to be equally strong when you are the center of attention or among the pack. Self-confident people do not need to brag or boast to be fulfilled. Self-confident people are not intimidated by hearing the opposing view. It is the inner strength and driving force allowing you to reach your personal best.

> *You never know who you will run into ... We were newlyweds living in Salt Lake and ready for a change! Marlon was accepted to a private architecture school in Southern California and I needed to find a job so that we could move out there and get on with our lives.*
>
> *I was interviewing in sales with many different medical companies and was just returning from a job interview with Johnson & Johnson in Seattle when I met a nicely-dressed man in the baggage claim area. I noticed his extremely cool basketball-style briefcase and just started asking some questions. (I was in the interview "mode.")*

He explained that he was a sales manager for Spalding Sports and was traveling to ride with some of his salespeople. I said great, then maybe you can interview me for a position with your company. He said he only had a sales opportunity that was coming available in the LA area. I said great, I was ready to relocate to that area and that it would be a perfect fit. I then continued the dialog, selling myself, knowing this was the job for me! I was fresh out of college with little sales experience, but I was hungry!

I continued the interview process meeting with a tough national sales manager and others from Chicopee, Mass. After a grueling interview process I was offered the job. I found out later that I had joined a "men's club" with only two women in the sales force and I was one of them! I loved the challenge. This was a great success for me to have the guts to ask for the job, get THE job, love the job and be one of the top five salespeople for all the years I spent with Spalding!

— Susan Steiner, Applause

I was first hired by News Corporation in 1990, right out of college, to work in the special projects group of Murdoch Magazines in New York City (a stable of consumer magazines then owned by Rupert Murdoch). My major had been psychology/pre-med, and I was eventually planning on going to medical school. I was hired by a combination of skill, luck, and contacts — like most people, I suppose.

When I arrived in New York, I found out that the woman who hired me to work for her had resigned. Instead of waiting for the powers that be to fill her role, I asked to take over her responsibilities. To my great surprise, they agreed with the condition that it be on a trial basis. After a year, I was still in the role, and went on to start one of the first consumer online services (using a technology based on Minitel services — a precursor to the Internet). It was called New York Magazine Online. I never did make it to medical school, but I enjoyed being a part of the birth of the Internet era.

— Melissa Grossman, freelance consultant

THE TIMES OF UNREALISTIC EXPECTATIONS

We live in a world that fantasizes over Hollywood and sets unrealistic expectations in the real world. Turn on the television; go to a movie theater, pick up a beauty magazine or read the latest success magazine and you will find tough acts to follow. Super heroes, super models, billionaires, and other forms of perfection have become the unattainable standard against which we measure ourselves.

Forget about all those extraordinary lifestyles and super sensational stories. The race is not against the people you see on television or read about in the magazines. The race in life is against yourself and the sooner you learn this lesson the better off you will be in life.

To race against yourself, it is essential to set goals and track your progress and have a real strong grasp of what you stand for, what is important in your life and how you want to be perceived.

IMPORTANCE OF CONFIDENCE

> **Your success depends mainly on yourself**
> **and whether you believe in yourself.**
> — *William J. H. Boeteker*

Have you ever seen an athlete go on a streak of success? A basketball player hits seven or eight shots in a row, a baseball player hits in 15 consecutive games or a hockey goalie becomes a virtual brick wall in net? There are an equal number of situations where the reverse prevails. We have seen great athletes go through extended periods of ineptitude and failure. We call these streaks or slumps, which can be largely explained by a person's level of self-confidence. It is no different in the work force than in sports, or even in social settings. Success, winning, and even luck come to those who are confident and believe in themselves. Confidence is the engine and driving force leading us toward the path of success.

When I was first promoted to sales manager at ADP, the other managers were responsible for selecting my team. You might be able to guess the quality of salespeople the managers were willing to offer up. This was not exactly an all-star cast. In fact, the entire team was created from people who had failed the previous year. One of my reps, Trisha Potochar, ended the previous year with a paltry 15% of quota. She was visibly nervous and uncomfortable in her role and strongly considering a career change out of sales. During my introductory interview with Trisha, I was pleasantly surprised to discover how much she knew about the products and her territory.

It became evident early on in the process that Trisha's major problem was not her sales ability, but her lack of confidence in her sales ability. The only training and coaching she needed was focusing on raising her confidence. Together we focused on all the positives and accentuated the things she felt comfortable with and positive about. We celebrated the early successes publicly and let her and everyone else know that she was on a great run and would be successful. Her confidence slowly built and began to change the way she called, pitched and closed. She went on to exceed her quota in 11 of the 12 months that fiscal year, reaching the prestigious President's Club. Twelve short months later, Trisha was promoted to a systems consultant.

In one year, she went from the worst performing rep in the region to being promoted to a prestigious position in the organization. When she started believing in herself and focusing on her strengths, you could see a gradual change in her demeanor. The better she felt about herself, the more interest she took in her job and her career began to flourish.

— *Eric J. Hinds*

When people believe in their ability, they work at a higher level and have more aptitude for success. Most people are insecure and uncertain about their abilities. Often times, positive reinforcement from someone else or the celebration of an early success will change the way we feel about ourselves and consequently help us to become more effective. Unfortunately, many people do not get the proper confidence builders or early recognition to develop and maintain that confidence.

SIGNS OF CONFIDENCE

Have you ever seen someone walk in the room and immediately capture the attention of the people in that room? These people have self-confidence and it shows through in the presence. Often times, it is almost as important to be able to carry yourself with confidence as it is to have confidence. Conveying confidence is a positive step toward developing confidence itself. The following are signs of confidence:

Walk Tall. Posture often tells the tale of a confident person. People who walk tall are often perceived to have higher self-confidence than those who slouch when they walk. A firm handshake when you are greeting someone will also exude confidence.

Eye Contact. Look people in the eye when you speak with them. Eye contact is another critical element in demonstrating self-confidence. When a person is talking to you and not looking you in the eye, it is often perceived that the person is uncomfortable or not telling the truth about something.

Laugh at Yourself. The true loud and clear sign that a person has self-confidence is when a person is comfortable enough to laugh at himself. Whether you make a mistake, trip up the stairs or are at the wrong end of a joke, ease the tension and smile.

Humble. Do not confuse confidence with cockiness. Being humble will go a long way in conveying confidence. Confident people do not have to beat their chests and yell, "I am the best."

Don't Be Defensive. If you are ever put on the spot, accused or backed into a corner, do not act defensively. A confident person is comfortable and in control.

Likability Quotient. Confident people often attract others. The likability is usually not easily explainable or clear.

Be Comfortable. Confident people do not always have to make a scene or put anyone down. A confident person is comfortable in approaching people and initiating contact. Confident people know their strengths and weaknesses.

SIGNS YOU ARE NOT CONFIDENT

A man's doubts and fears are his worst enemies.
— *William Wrigley Jr.*

There are an equal number of signs and actions that deliver the message that a person is not confident.

Slumped Shoulder. Slumped shoulders and a poor posture will convey the message that you do not have a lot of confidence.

Shuffling Feet. Pick up your feet when you walk. Shuffling feet shows a lack of interest in life and a person in need of a pick-me-up.

Avoiding Eye Contact. Look people in the eyes when you talk with them.

Speaking Out of Turn. At work, home or in the community, it is important to speak when you have something to contribute to the conversation. Do not speak just to hear your own voice. People who are unsure of themselves often speak too much and at the wrong time.

Arrogant Attitude. Sometimes arrogance can hide a person who is not confident. Do not let this become your game. People do not like arrogant people.

Defensive, Nervous, Uncomfortable and Indecisive. These are not characteristics you want next to a list describing you and how you act toward others. If any of these adjectives have been used to describe you, it is important to focus on changing the perception as well as the reality.

Trapped in the Comfort Zone. People who lack confidence often appear trapped in their own comfort zone. This prevents them from meeting new people, adopting new ideas or making changes in their lifestyle.

HOW TO ACHIEVE CONFIDENCE

Confidence is not something you are born with or something you acquire with the wave of a magic wand. Self-confidence is a product of your environment and something you can and should develop. The following steps are guidelines that will improve your confidence:

IMPORTANCE OF THE ENVIRONMENT

It is essential to put yourself in an environment in which you can be successful. To do this, you must have a good indication of the situations where you are most comfortable. Would you be better in a large company environment or a small, more personable one? Are you more effective in a corporate America atmosphere or one that is much more casual? Are you a self-starter or would you prefer a more extensive training program? Do you work well under pressure in a high-energy environment or are you better in a softer, more relaxed atmosphere? The answers to these questions are crucial, because of the direct effect on the confidence you carry into that job.

If you grew up in a small mid-western town with a close-knit family and attended the University of Nebraska majoring in agriculture, you have to be very confident to take a job on Wall Street in New York City. It might be better to start with a job closer to home or in a smaller city. The more you understand about yourself, the better you will be able to recognize a situation where you will be comfortable, confident and successful.

Eric interned at Merrill Lynch in college and had a great experience. Unfortunately, he was uncomfortable talking to people about money at age 22. Eric had never worked in a corporate environment and thought he needed some personal development and a slower introduction into the real world. After careful and extensive research he identified the sales companies with the top training programs. ADP provided the environment, training, recognition and all the support he needed to succeed right out of college.

Eric needed more from the organization and probably would not have done too well. ADP was a competitive place filled with young people, which directed a less formal environment. Choosing the right place allowed him to be comfortable and confident, which led to an environment to be successful. Your confidence plays a huge role in your ability to get your job done so do not choose an environment that could in any fashion put a damper on your confidence.

ACCENTUATE YOUR STRENGTHS

When you enter the work force, your first goal should be to keep your work life fairly simple. Although you might have a burning desire to take on the world, it is important to understand what you do well and concentrate on getting some early wins. First impressions are crucial and will set the tone for your level of confidence. It is important to excel during your first few weeks on your first major project and in your first meeting. Often times, people will make decisions regarding your competence very quickly so remember that on your early assignments. An early success can boost your confidence and start you on the right track.

> *My first ADP training session included a role-playing exercise in front of the entire group. The first couple of days I remained on the quiet side. I was just waiting for the right opportunity. When the facilitator asked for two volunteers, I knew it was my chance. I loved to speak in front of groups and jumped at the chance. I put on quite an entertaining exhibition and was widely complimented by my peers. With every compliment, I could feel my confidence level rise.*

> — *Eric J. Hinds*

It is important to recognize what you do well and stick to your strengths, especially early on in a new situation, when your confidence level will not be sky high. There is nothing more motivational or better for your confidence than positive recognition. If you have the opportunity to shine, the effect on your confidence can be very positive.

SPEND TIME WITH THE RIGHT PEOPLE

Spend as much time as possible with people who make you feel good about yourself. These people are friends who know when to pick you up and make you feel good. These people have a genuine interest in seeing you happy and walking tall. The more positive energy, compliments and lifts you have around you, the higher your confidence level will become.

> *I was a young sales rep and had just won my first big deal. My competitor saw me in the hall of the customer and congratulated me. He was probably in his 50s while I was in my early 20s. He called me and offered to buy me lunch. We had competed against one another for about a year and didn't have much of a relationship other than seeing each other at customer accounts. He took me to lunch and we had a good conversation. He asked me about the deal that I just won (FYI, I had a signed contract). I told him the price that I won the deal at. Within hours of our lunch my competitor went back to the customer and undercut my price on the deal. The customer, lacking business ethics and integrity, decided to take the new deal and did not honor the contract that we had. The lesson: Not everyone has the same integrity that you do. Some people will do whatever it takes to win a deal regardless of the ethical nature of that act.*

> — *Todd Nelson, E Plus*

Avoid People Who Put You Down

This includes people who call you fat, stupid or incompetent. Equally important is what people do not say. Spend less time with people who make you feel less adequate. This goes beyond work into life. If this is how your friends communicate to each other, find new friends.

Listen

Direction and guidance provided by someone you respect and like will help build your confidence. Find older and successful people to take stock in your development and progress. Listen to their advice and take it to heart.

Work Hard

The work praises the man.

— *Irish Proverb*

I always hated the advice of work very hard, learn as much as you can and your break will come, but in my 10 years of work experience, that has turned out to be the best advice — shut up and work.
— *Jerome Hepplemen, PBHGF Funds*

There is no substitute for working hard. After a hard day's work, when you gave it your all, you will feel more confidence in yourself and your work. Hard work might entail preparing for a big presentation or staying late working on a big project. That hard work will pay off when the moment of truth comes and you have done all you could have done.

It was the summer of 1996 and I was a recently hired New Jersey Nets corporate sales account executive (fancy term for ticket sales guy). The Nets were coming off another dazzling 30-52 season and there was not a lot of love in New Jersey for the Swamp Dragons. Throughout our daily cold calls we would have stories of being laughed at, cursed at, or simply hung up on. As any good rookie would do, I sat there with my index cards full of rebuttals to the resounding NO that was sure to come on most calls. One day I found myself on the phone with J&G cleaning just waiting for the opportunity to utilize one of my index cards. The owner came back with the good old, "I don't have time in my day for a meeting." Lucky for me that was covered on index card #3. I couldn't wait to get my response out, "What time do you start your day and how do you like your coffee? I will meet you in the parking lot of your office and walk you to the front door. If you like what I have to say you will invite me in for a meeting. If not you will have a free cup of coffee."

The client came back with an okay, and I almost fell off my chair! This actually works. Little did I know what J and G cleaning actually did; they cleaned sheets for hotels and restaurants. The client then dropped the hammer, "I start my day at 4:30 a.m., see you then!" I woke myself up at 3:30 a.m. for the trip to Bloomfield, N.J., and was about 15 minutes early. The owner arrived around 4:35 a.m. and laughed as he stepped out of his car. He gave me the time and eventually became a New Jersey Nets full season ticket holder.

— Brian Cull, Major League baseball

I was working for the Cavaliers right out of school as a sales rep and thought I had the dream job, in my hometown, my favorite team, favorite sport. Life was good. My boss tells me to go interview for a job with an executive recruiting firm that specializes in the sports industry. Said it would be good for my career. I couldn't understand why. I put my best suit on and headed for the interview. I find myself a few weeks later working for Buffy Filippell who runs TeamWork Consulting. At the time her business operated out of her house (the basement of it) and it was a three-person operation: me, Buffy and an intern. It didn't take long for me to ask myself, "What the heck am I doing here?"

Buffy was a 100% pure perfectionist. Her name was on the business and it was her way or the highway. I had never met someone so direct with criticism when it wasn't done right. I knew I was in for some tough times. Her expectation of workload was beyond what I could have imagined. I knew work ethic through sports but never expected to apply such grit, determination and hours toward a job in business. It was THAT important to Buffy. As I struggled through the many mistakes and corrections from Buffy I often thought about quitting. I wasn't happy, did not enjoy the day-to-day environment and workload, and was struggling with not being headed back to campus in the fall.

What I realized during these trying times was that I made a commitment to the industry and to myself to make this work. I looked at the learning experience I was being provided and what the long-term positives could be if I stuck with it. Buffy was tough, but she also cared about me and my personal success. This was a relationship worth working on. I put my head down and worked typically from 7:45 a.m. to 9:00 p.m. I developed a work ethic I've found matched by very few since. I networked in the industry like no other opportunity could have provided.

After two years Buffy worked hard to provide me with several good opportunities with sports teams and I chose to go work for the Detroit Pistons. So far I've met most of my career path goals and feel they could not have been accomplished without the wonderful opportunity I had at Teamwork. Buffy Filippell and I now have a wonderful business and personal relationship.

Morale of the story…"Tough times don't last, tough people do." When you think you want to give up, you need to look around and see if you're giving up on something that could be the best thing for you in the long run. Who knows where I would be if I had quit? I know for sure, staying at Teamwork and working through those difficult times was the best decision I could have made early in my career.

— *Chad Estis, Gund Arena Company/ Cleveland Cavaliers*

REVIEW SUCCESS STORIES

Go to the library or bookstore and pick up books about successful people who have overcome tremendous odds to reach success. Reading these compelling stories will help you see that most of these people are no different from you and overcame tremendous odds to reach their place in the sun.

What one can do so can another.
— *Anthony Hopkins, "The Edge"*

READ "THE MAGIC OF BELIEVING"

Read the book, "The Magic of Believing," by Claude Bristol. The book extols the virtue and power of the human mind and its potential. It is a book that explains how strong beliefs will bring rewards beyond your imagination. This is the essence of confidence.

AVOID THE CLIFF

It is as proper to have pride in oneself as it is ridiculous to show it to others.
— *Francois de LaRochefoucauld*

There is a fine line between confidence and cockiness. The key to success in the business world is to walk to the edge of that cliff of confidence without falling over the edge into cockiness. A confident person believes and trusts in his own ability and is willing to listen to sound advice and counsel, while knowing skills and talents should always be developed. Confident people are well liked and attract others to them. When you fall over the cliff, you are losing the edge you need to be successful. The cocky or arrogant person stops reaching for a higher plateau, believing he has already reached the pinnacle. Arrogance is a people repellent.

In 1992, I was a 22-year-old researcher for ESPN's Up Close, the network's daily talk show. It was my job to get all of the background information on each guest and to develop a line of questioning that would serve as the foundation of the interview. It was a great job. Every day sports celebrities would come in and, in a way, I would get to ask them whatever I wanted. We had 260 shows a year and averaged two guests per show so there was a lot of fact finding to do.

Just prior to the 1992 Women's Basketball Final Four, we had Ann Meyers, a broadcaster covering the game, on the show. I did not know a thing about women's basketball so I asked a friend a mine what would make for interesting conversation. He told me that a pair of twins who played collegiately posed for "Playboy." He was unsure what team they played for but it was a team from the southeast. In addition, I heard that a pair of twins were the best players for Virginia, a team in the Final Four. Virginia is in the southeast. Sort of. I figured they were the same pair because what would be the odds of there being two twins in college basketball at major programs in the southeast. I thought it would be interesting to get Ann's take on whether that was good for college basketball and to get insight on these twins who were talented enough to lead a team to the Final Four while attractive enough to pose for "Playboy."

Ann was asked the question and looks confused. She said on the air, "Are you sure this is correct?" The host looked over to me and I nodded yes. The show aired 24 hours later. We received hundreds of telephone calls from angry Virginia fans. The twins who posed for "Playboy" were from LSU. One of the calls came from the Virginia twins who were stunned and demanded a retraction. The next show led off with the retraction. It was embarrassing for the network. The host. For me. I wrote a long letter to the twins apologizing. It was a very costly error and a terrible mistake. It taught me the lesson, however, to make sure that every fact was double-checked.

— Jason Schirn, Hager Pacific

"Like any kid coming straight out of college I thought I knew everything and wanted to show the old school folks at my Fortune 500 company that there is a new way to do things. After a large string of successes as a financial analyst and a burgeoning ego, I found out that I was less than perfect. My manager had given me the responsibility of creating the "foils" (read: PowerPoint slides printed on transparency paper for the old school VPs) for the quarterly financial review. Out of the 40-plus graphs that I created, one had what I recognized as a minor error once it hit the overhead projector. Needless to say, it was a grave error that changed the complete annual forecast. One of the VPs whom I presumed to be "clueless" caught the error *immediately and my manager took the fall for me.*

After the meeting, my manager explained that everyone makes mistakes and to not worry about it. However, within the week I created a book entry as a debit vs. credit or a credit vs. a debit (I don't remember) that was a mistake to the tune of $1 million. That error was so significant that our sector earnings had to be restated to WALL STREET. Once I had endured the worst week of my limited career, I created a folder called "Lapses in Greatness" in part to keep my ego in check and to remind myself that I still had a lot to learn. I am happy to say that the folder still exists and entries to it are few and far between."

— Michael Zaharis, Accenture

Don't Let Them See You Sweat

You will find yourself in numerous uncomfortable situations in a new job. It is important to try to maintain your composure and professionalism at all times. Do your best to learn from the experiences and file them away in your head so you do not get caught in the same situation again.

As an experienced sales executive, I rarely lost my confidence in front of clients or a potential prospect. I have been on thousands of sales calls. The first week after arriving at my new job I was gung-ho and ready to go. I made the mistake of prematurely setting up sales calls with some of my top prospects.

I honestly felt that I had an advantage over the others in my starting class because of my previous sales experience and success. I knew I didn't know the ins and outs of our products, but was overconfident that my sales ability would carry me through. I have never been more wrong (or humiliated) in my life. I arrived at the business of a family friend looking to sell a 401(k) program. The questions seemed to attack like missiles and I began to lose my confidence. My ego would not let me cut bait. I froze and lost complete control of the call. I was not prepared enough in the new field to shoot from the hip and my overconfidence in my sales ability cost me a 401(k) sale.

— Eric J. Hinds

When I was 23 and finishing my internship with IMG, I made plans to fly

Chapter 8

Manage Your Boss

Seek first to understand, then to be understood.

— *Steven Covey*

to Florida and visit a friend. He said he could get me a meeting with Gary Player Inc. and the PGA while I was in town. I decided to try for another meeting with Greg Norman's company to meet his agent. I call Frank Williams and ask his assistant for a meeting because I would be in town meeting with the PGA and would like to stop over. She said, "Who is this?" To which I respond, "Casey Murray with IMG." (Williams used to work for IMG and left to start to manage Norman exclusively. So the assistant called me back and said he would meet me.

Everything looked great until a week before the meeting she called and said Mr. Williams would like to know what this meeting is for. I said to discuss business ideas and to better understand his business. She said fine, we will see you next week. Moral of the story, it pays to ask for something you want. I had a great meeting and to this day I always get a chuckle thinking how I talked myself in there.

A side note: At the meeting, when he realized I was fishing for a job and I had offered to carry Greg Norman's luggage, he said "Hell, you're only 23 – go make some money for IMG. They will hire you. Get after it. If you are going fail, fail big and go after it. By the way, what do they think of me over at IMG?"

— Casey Murray, ROI Consultants

This rat race is not a smooth and slow ride in the right lane. This race is filled with bumps, dangerous curves, fallen branches, a driving rainstorm and many other unforeseen obstacles. Confidence will help you navigate comfortably and safely through the decision points you will come across in your life. Be proactive in identifying what helps you feel confident and put yourself in those situations more often. Confidence can and should be developed. Believe in your strengths!

Hopefully your confidence level is moving up, because you are going to need it to manage your boss effectively. While this concept seems strange initially, it is both possible and necessary to manage your boss. The relationship with your supervisor can take many shapes and forms. In most instances your boss will have influence over promotions, raises and your ultimate success. The more proactive you can be in managing this relationship, the more quickly you will find success in the workplace.

Discovering Expectations

The first week on the job is usually an unsettling, uneasy time. Some organizations will have first-class training programs, a quality orientation program or other ways to make your first week palatable. Unfortunately, many of you may just be escorted to your cubicle with no formal orientation. Most of you will merely be given a phone, pencil, and password to your computer and a mere wish of luck, which you will certainly need.

You will be very anxious your first week worrying about the basics: Are you wearing the right clothes? Arriving at the right time? Or simply trying to figure out when and where to go to lunch. What time should you go home at night? Is there an office alarm and if so how do you set it? What is the password to your computer? Where do you get pens, paper, etc.? How do you set up your voice mail? E-mail? Blue Cross or US Healthcare? 401(k), what is 401(k)? It can and will seem overwhelming in a new job.

You are better off trying to solve world hunger than trying to make an impact at work your first couple of weeks. It is a difficult time and you must be patient. The key is to try to be as perceptive as possible to figure out what is expected of you.

What Makes the Boss Tick?

Through all of your uncertainties and anxieties, it is important to comb through it all in an attempt to find what your boss expects of you. Remember to keep your priorities straight. Near the top of the list is keeping the boss happy. Your boss's happiness will to a large extent dictate your happiness and success on the job. It is more important than your health care plan or setting up your 401(k) or any other human resources issue that might seem important to others.

Find out what is important to your boss. There are a number of questions you need to have answered. What will help your boss look good, help get you promoted or get a big raise? How is your boss evaluated? How will your boss evaluate you? In what way could you help your boss? You need to find out what your boss's hot buttons are. Probe to find out what is important and what drives the person.

Scott had three different bosses, each of whom had different hot buttons and priorities. The first wanted to be humored, patronized and taken care of at all cost. His shirts had to be medium starched and boxed, and picked up every Tuesday, Scott knew because he made the trip to the cleaner's each week. His letters had to be typed a certain way with specific spacing, fonts and verbiage. The second wanted someone he could develop and someone who would run through a wall for him. He wanted a protégé, someone who talked like he did, dressed like he did and thought like he did. He never wanted to be questioned. He wanted action. The third boss wanted sales and protocol, in that order. The only thing he wanted to hear was that Scott had landed a big deal or set up appointments or made his cold calls. For each one, it took time and energy to find their hot buttons.

My second year at Cendant I was promoted to run a division with 130 employees. It was a major jump since I went from sales to running an operation. I poured my heart into the job. Most days I worked from 7a.m. to 9 p.m. I was a total animal ... so I thought.

At the time I was working for a director who was very different from me. She was a process engineering type who demanded that her managers understand the process. I was a sales guy who tried to influence people with my attitude. Even though I heard her, I never listened and continued to think that all my energy could overcome my lack of understanding the process.

At my annual review I was certain that I would get a great one since my effort was exceptional, even though my results had been mediocre. All I could think was, someone has to see how hard I am working and will reward me for it. I received my review and it was awful. I was ranked below average for the first time in my career.

Bottom line, I did not listen to what my boss wanted, which was process maps. She did not care if I came in at 10 a.m. or 4 p.m., she just wanted to understand the process. Today, I do a much better job at asking my boss to define the specific goals I need to meet. Once they commit to it in writing, it helps me maintain focus, while giving my boss control over the outcome.

— *Scott Stork, Cendant*

Don't Be Intimidated

Leave your security blanket at home and come in with a strong determination. Do not let an overpowering attitude or a boss with a strong personality back you and your ideas down. But, let's not fool ourselves. The phrase, "The boss is always right" is often times a reality. Understand the mentality and ego that comes along with titles and experience. Most bosses want you and everybody else to know and accept who is the boss. However, a good boss does not want a puppet, a yes man or non-thinker. A self-starter who can work independently and voice opinions professionally is a hot commodity and is a valuable part of the team.

As discussed in the previous chapter, confidence will distinguish you from your peers. Confidence is displayed by the ability to wrap your arms around an idea, initiate and encourage discussion about the idea, make the right decision, live with the consequences and have the ability to get right back on the horse again with a new idea or program. There is no greater way to get respect in an organization than to demonstrate confidence.

Confidence is not about always being right, it is the willingness to be wrong.

> During my first year as a supply officer on the USS McKee, I learned a valuable lesson about CYA. One of my many duties at the time was being the officer in charge of the ship's post office. I had about five postal clerks who did the real work. My job was to ensure integrity of the accountability (count stamps and money) and adherence to postal guidelines. I had what I thought was a luxury in my lead postal clerk, who has served for nearly 20 years.
>
> One afternoon, after the post office shut down for the day, my lead clerk called me up to let me know that a few money order vouchers were missing. She assured me that she was properly handling the reporting for this "minor" mistake by the clerk who had been conducting business that day. This is when, "Houston, we have a problem" should have been blaring in my head from the training I had received on the potential pitfalls of dealing with money orders, but I was headed out of town that evening for some much deserved leave, and I had what turned out to be blind faith in my lead postal clerk's expertise. Mistake. Three months later, Navy postal inspectors showed up at the ship with documents indicating that the three money orders had been cashed for the maximum amount, and surprise, surprise, there was never any money paid to match the cashing.

The postal service wanted its money, and my boss wanted somebody's ass, mostly mine, since I had never informed him of the missing vouchers. Well, shit rolls down hill, so my lead postal clerk took the brunt of the ass chewing (junior officers are expected to screw up). Fortunately, we did determine that one of my subordinate postal clerks was a crook after several weeks of investigation. My take from this experience could have easily been to not trust my subordinates, but that is not an effective way to lead or manage. I did take away some things that helped me during the rest of my career in the Navy.

1. Know the rules, or know where to find the rules. Nobody expected me to know every detail about running the post office, but it was sure as hell my responsibility to make sure we did things by the book. Ask lots of questions until you are confident that you have done the right thing;

2. Always keep the chain of command informed, especially when the news is bad. Better to present a problem when it is small and manageable that when it has turned into a huge mess (postal inspectors investigating your accountability is no fun).

— Chad Duhon, FUQUA graduate student

PICK YOUR SPOTS

The best poker players in the world know how to read people. We are creatures of habit and great poker players are students of human behavior. Do your eyes light up with a good hand? Do you talk more when you think you can win? Are you twitching your fingers before you fold? Are betting tendencies predictable or do they have just the right mix? We are not suggesting you take up poker and become a card shark, but this illustration does point out the importance of being able to read your boss and react appropriately.

Make your best effort to understand the type of mood your boss is in at various times. It is important to understand when she may be more likely to turn a request down without consideration or simply approve any and every request that is made. Learn to read the different cues your boss will give off. Does the person smile all the time or just when she is very happy? Does your boss look down before bad news or close the door when there is a problem? Be aware and make note of the different reactions to different situations. Be able to predict the upper brass reactions and responses and act accordingly. This will not happen overnight. Depending on your level of access, awareness and your boss's mannerisms, you should be up to speed in about six months.

ADP roll call was a weekly update on where the sales force stood as compared to the region's goals. If the weekly numbers were good, the general manager was very happy. A good week would bring an upbeat tone in the office, smiles all around and a sense of positive energy. If the numbers were bad, the general manager was not happy. The general manager would often increase demands, inspections and control — and that would lead to a feeling of uneasiness and tension around the office.

Gary Johnson, a mid-level manager, was an expert at reading the general manager's emotions. He often would time his special requests, additional contests and rewards for weeks when the region was exceeding sales and flying high. Gary always seemed to have his requests granted. Poor timing and even worse delivery plagued the other managers, who often made the requests after a sub-par week or without regard to the mood of the office. Gary's year-end entertainment budget line would exceed that of the other four managers combined.

> My first boss was a real piece of work. I showed up for my first day. My orientation consisted of, "Here's a stack of leads, young guy, now go out and start selling." I knew I had a tough road ahead. At that time, to make a little more money, I doubled duties as the team's public relations manager. To not let this interfere with my selling, I always worked on the PR portion of the job at night. Still, being single and not having a life, I had plenty of time on my hands.

> However, working one night, I was startled to see the GM in my door way. He asked a question. To this day, I can't remember the question. I think it had something to do with the media guide. Well, he obviously didn't like my answer because he had a stack of papers in his hands and just blew up like a volcano. He swore, threw the papers all over my office and carried on for 10 minutes (at the time it seemed like 30 minutes). I was shocked. I had never had anyone treat me like this in the workplace. I recounted the story to my mentor at the time. He too, was shocked; however he gave me a great bit of advice. He said, "You know how you felt when the General Manager did that to you." I said I did. He said, "Now, when you start to manage people, you know how not to manage them. You have just been given an important lesson in management, how not to do it."

> — David Cohen, Atlanta Falcons

POLITICS IN BUSINESS

Look at the president of the company. Did the person come up through the ranks of marketing? Sales? Operations? Manufacturing? This will tell a big story about where the emphasis of the company is. It is also important to understand the career lines of the different personnel you are in touch with. Get to know the history of the company and who played the biggest roles in the company's development.

There is a political ring around every company. Who knows who is important. This information will help you make small talk with the big executives while showing an interest in them and their careers. The more questions you ask to gain a better understanding of those around you, the better prepared you will be to manage those on the upper rungs of the corporate ladder.

SPENDING QUALITY TIME WITH THE BIG CHEESE

There will be so many things going through your head you might forget the most important task your first week. It is crucial to schedule a mutually convenient time to sit down with your boss in the latter part of the week. Offer to come in early or stay late to accommodate the boss's schedule. If there is more than one boss, attempt to schedule a joint meeting.

Satisfaction is directly correlated to expectations. To satisfy your boss, you need to meet expectations. To meet those expectations, you first must know what is expected of you. If possible, try to get quantifiable results that will make your boss happy. Try to break the expectations into daily, weekly, monthly and yearly goals.

The objective is to get specific information about what your boss expects of you. Prior to the meeting, prepare a list of questions to review in the meeting. Use the list below as a starting point to the job.

What are your expectations this year in terms of specific goals, achievement milestones, etc. you are looking for me to accomplish?

Listen for signals or signs. Often times it is important to develop follow-up questions from the response. Specific information will provide you with a measuring stick. The more specific the information, the better off you will be.

What was your career path that led you into your current position? Tell me about your career.

Everyone has an ego. People like to talk about themselves and this question will provide another forum for them. More importantly, however, it will help you get a better understanding of where the person is coming from, where the person places emphasis and what you will need to do to satisfy the person's needs. This question often helps the person to feel less threatened and drop his guard. The more comfortable the person is with you, the more likely you will get straightforward and truthful answers.

What is the most important thing I am responsible for in this job?

This is asked to try to find hot buttons. This will give a good indication of where you should pay special attention. Always look to follow up with questions that are thoughtful and reasonable.

How should I prioritize my daily activities?

> **Set priorities for your goals. A major part of successful living lies in the ability to put first things first. Indeed, the reason most major goals are not achieved is that we spend our time doing second things first.**
> — *Robert McKain*

This will help you identify which tasks are more important and should receive attention first. The only way to manage your boss is to understand what is important. Part of this process will allow you to over-deliver on the priorities and consequently gain increased confidence and autonomy.

What did the person in this position before me do that you liked? Didn't like?

If you listen closely, these questions will tell you a lot about what is important, what the real expectations are, and what actions and activities to avoid. This is a time to probe and ask for specific examples of the positive and the negative. Recognize the fact that the boss did not like the fact that the person was coming late to work and taking two-hour lunches. This is a clear message to beat your boss to the office each morning and eat lunch at your desk in 20 minutes or on the run. Pay special attention if the person in the position prior to you got promoted. This is a person you want to meet. It would also be important to discover what the boss's perception of the person is.

What would I have to do through the course of the year for you to consider it a great year?

This is sending a message to your boss that you are looking to make an impact and do a great job. It is also setting the bar and providing you a target to shoot for over the course of the year. If you do not know where the target is, shooting becomes increasingly difficult.

Are there specific things I can do to be more successful?

Here you are looking for tidbits, the little things that will push you over the top. For example, make 100 phone calls each day, get in at 7:00 a.m., etc.

Who is the most successful person in a similar job? And what do you think makes that person successful?

This will give you a role model after which to pattern your behavior. It also might be an opportunity to approach the most successful person and ask a similar line of questions. It might be beneficial to spend a day or two with this person. A compliment or two will go a long way in having this person willing to help you.

The answers to these questions will help you navigate through the rough waters and difficult decisions about priorities that you will have to make. Hopefully your boss will be the type of person you can learn from and someone who will invest in your future. The ideal supervisor is one who derives pleasure from your success, wants to see you succeed and will help you along the path. This scheduled meeting has already put you at the head of the class, but it is just the beginning. Do not drop the ball.

Follow up Regularly

At the conclusion of the meeting, ask your supervisor if he/she would be comfortable having monthly meetings to check on your progress. This will also provide a time to have the boss provide you some feedback and suggestions for improvement. It will also provide the opportunity to ask any questions or bring up any challenges you may be facing. Remember, your boss has most likely been in your position before and can help you with the routine problems you have encountered. It also sends a message that you are encouraging feedback.

Most organizations have formalized reviews for employees. Unfortunately, most of these reviews take place once a year. This is not a trap you want to fall into in your job. The more scheduled, organized and check-up meetings with your manager, the less chance of you being surprised in your review. This is a chance to evaluate your performance along the way and make the necessary changes if they need to happen or simply continue doing the things that are positive.

Get the meetings on your calendar. With the increasing pace of business and rapid changes taking place in the marketplace, everyone's schedules seem to be tighter and planned further out in the future. It is best if these meetings are scheduled regularly and in both of your calendars.

One-on-One

Informal contact and ensuing conversation is at least as important as the formal prescheduled meetings. Usually you can find your boss in the office before most in the morning and after most have left for the day in the evening. What a great opportunity for you! The informal communication you will have during the off hours at the office will provide you unparalleled access and undivided attention. There is a lot less activity during these off-peak times and the boss usually feels less encumbered with the day's activities. This time is priceless and well spent.

Respect Your Boss's Time

Nothing in business is so valuable as time.
— *John H. Patterson*

Time is money in the business world. It is important to pick your spots with your boss and make sure that the time together will be well spent.

> *I have always been overly aggressive as a salesperson. When I was hired by the Philadelphia Eagles to sell tickets and luxury boxes, I knew this was my shot at the big time. I would work harder and longer than anyone else. I had taken the boss on two appointments already, neither of which panned out.*
>
> *I took my boss on a third appointment and it was a disaster. We were running late and I tried to make up for lost time by driving like a mad man. My boss looked scared to death — he was holding on for dear life. After driving for more than an hour, we arrived 20 minutes late because I had not taken the time to get the proper directions and was pulled over for speeding on the way. The third meeting never materialized. We arrived only to find the people we were supposed to meet with were not available. These were squandered opportunities and a colossal waste of time, which made me look bad in front of my boss, again.*
>
> *On the way back from the third meeting, I could sense my boss was*

going to read me the riot act. Instead, he asked me if I would like some feedback. He told me it was important to be proactive and consider how some of these mishaps could be prevented in the future. I should have called ahead for directions (or at least checked mapquest.com), called to confirm the meetings and left early enough to get to the appointment on time. I vowed that would never happen to me again.

— Shayne Donohue, Philadelphia Eagles

Unfortunately, our next sales appointment together would be even worse...

The office manager sent an office-wide memo via e-mail reading: The office will be closed this Friday in observance of Good Friday. Enjoy the long weekend!

I rushed into my office disheveled and frustrated. I had scheduled a huge meeting with EDS, a multi-billion dollar company on Friday and wanted the boss to attend the meeting with me. The boss agreed to come in on Friday only after he was assured the meeting was confirmed and I had the directions down pat.

We met at the office early Friday morning and my boss could see the excitement and anticipation in my eyes. My first big appointment with the boss. It was going to be great. As we got closer to the company address, I started to sense a problem. The neighborhood was just too residential to house a multi-billion dollar company. I was right. EDS was actually Ed's Auto Body. We met with the president and owner (Ed, who was also the chief mechanic). Unfortunately, Ed insisted on welding while we presented the material. It was a tough ride back to the office.

— Shayne Donohue, Philadelphia Eagles

Do everything you can to avoid embarrassing situations like this for yourself or some day when you really need the boss to be there, he might not be as willing. Shayne had a rough start with his boss at the Eagles. Despite all this, he is very successful at the Eagles through a combination of hard work and single mindedness, but it took his boss longer to have confidence and trust in Shayne's ability to be successful.

THE POWER OF THE PEN

This one is going to take some time, effort and thought. You will also need to be organized and consistent. At the end of the initial meeting suggest that you would like to turn in a timely written recap, detailing your activities over a specified period of time — a week, month, quarter, etc. The report should be in summary form and be limited to one page. You are looking to demonstrate you are together, working hard and looking for feedback.

> *I had a lot of difficulty communicating with my first boss at the Nets. I never knew what to say to him and I overanalyzed everything he said to me. I felt like I was back in junior high. So I decided to start writing a report each week to let him know what I was working on. I would drop them in his in-box each Friday before I left for the weekend. The great thing about the Friday Report (as he called it) was that it opened up the lines of communication and eliminated my uncomfortableness around him.*

> *— Scott M. O'Neil*

The work week is hectic and fast paced. It is tough for supervisors to fully comprehend all the work you are doing. The report is a tool to provide evidence and examples of exactly what you are working on should be designed to help your boss' perception of you and your work. It also provides an opportunity for your boss to help on a particular thing that catches his eye, where he might be able to save you some time and effort.

For example, I used a weekly report, deemed the Friday Report, which looked something like this:

Cold Calls Made This Week: 329

Meetings Set Up:

Schering Plough	Jan 3	10:00
Bob's Stores	Jan 3	11:00
Modell's	Jan 3	1:30
Texaco	Jan 3	2:45
Fred's Auto Body	Jan 4	9:30
Mel's Diner	Jan 4	10:30
Aamco	Jan 4	2:00
Coca-Cola Bottling	Jan 4	3:30
Sprint	Jan 5	9:00

Frito Lay	Jan 5	4:00
Sands	Jan 5	6:00
Ford Motor Credit	Jan 6	10:00
Sal's Pizzeria	Jan 6	11:00

Deals Closed this Week

Sheraton	$130,000
Britches	$67,500

Top Ten Prospects

1. **Chrysler** — Proposal in hand. Very interested, meeting next week.

2. **Sanyo** — Waiting to make sure the money is not cut from the budget.

3. **J. Crew** – Perfect fit for our audience. Director of marketing loved it. Need to present to VP next week.

4. **Brita** — New campaign to start in March. They have money, I just have to find out who can spend it.

5. **Huffman Koos** — Great meeting with president. He wants to work with us. Follow-up meeting toward end of the month.

6. **Very Fine** — My brother-in-law's father works here and has been a great internal coach. Hoping to have decision next week.

7. **Nissan** — The agency is recommending to the dealers association at the next meeting.

8. **Jackson-Cross** — Could use help with this one. Were very hot and recently cooled off and not sure why or what I should do about it.

9. **Ikea** — We have never had much success with them in past. However, there is a new marketing person and she seems interested.

10. **Pizza Hut** — Hoping for the contract back late today.

Handling the Formal Review Process

All companies have varying formal review processes. It is important to understand the process and how its results will affect you. Is the review process written and kept on file? Who has access to the completed review? Do you get a chance to grade yourself as well? Is the review process tied to your compensation? Is there a formal grade system? Does the review affect future opportunities to get promoted?

The answers to these questions will change the way you approach the process. If you do not know the answers, make sure you ask questions. These are answers you will need.

Spend significant time preparing for this session. Regardless of whether this is required or not, rate yourself in each category you will be graded on by your boss. It may be necessary to request a copy of the form from your boss or an office assistant. This self-analysis will provide a great starting point for discussion. Provide specific examples where you feel appropriate in evaluating your performance. Attempt to look at yourself, your behavior and your work as objectively as possible. If you have a good friend at work, ask the person for some feedback on specific aspects of your performance.

Where there is a divergence of the grades for each category between you and your boss, spend extra time discussing the topic. Spend more time on the grades that are less than stellar. Ask for specific examples and suggestions for ways to improve and do not get defensive.

No Formal Process. Now What?

If no formal review process exists, you want to do your best to create a more planned and prepared session with your direct supervisor. Target this effort twice a year. Make sure you approach your boss to give her plenty of prior notice and let her know you would like to sit down and discuss specific things you could improve on. Also, indicate you would like to have a thorough analysis, good and bad, of your job to date. Initially this will be awkward and uncomfortable; however it will get easier in time.

Boss Appreciation Day

People spend time and energy trying to look good in front of the boss and trying to impress the boss, but do not forget to say thanks. It is very important to express your gratitude for the effort your boss puts forth to help you in your career. Speak highly of

Chapter 9

Constructing and Delivering the Message

You are the message.

— Roger Ailes

your boss in front of your peers and other managers. This will go a long way and reflect positively on you as well.

> *My first job out of school was conducting research in a pharmaceutical lab at J&J. I loved the work and was learning every day. It was a great job and I was fortunate to have a supervisor who became my mentor, career advisor and most importantly, a friend.*
>
> *I left for grad school a few years later, but always stayed in touch with my old boss. Two years later he handed me a job in another department of J&J. We would go to lunch every couple of weeks and talk about our future, personal goals, professional goals and anything else that came up.*
>
> *He accepted a job with Astra Zeneca and saw a great opportunity for me. He knew my career aspirations were always to have my own business. There was consulting work his new company needed and he offered me the opportunity to start my own consulting company and win the contract. I did and Walker Health was born. I now employ 16 people and have secured additional contracts.*
>
> *It was my understanding of the importance of establishing and maintaining a relationship that opened doors for me throughout my career. It does not just happen. I had to work at building and maintaining the relationship.*
>
> *— Jim Walker*

Understand what is expected of you, follow through on expectations and processes to be successful, analyze the culture and how you can positively impact it and proactively recognize the help and support you receive along the way.

Constructing and communicating the proper message is another key to success in the rat race. This chapter will walk you through an effective communication model called the Arrow Theory and take you on a tour of the five senses and impart their impact on your grind to the top.

BE PART OF THE SOLUTION AND STOP BEING PART OF THE PROBLEM

The founders of T.O.G, a leadership and quality training and consulting company, created the Arrow Theory. T.O.G. has worked around the world with management teams of McDonalds, Xerox, Kodak, Texaco, and ADP among others. They found the most effective way to teach the managers to communicate more effectively and reduce the amount of hurt in the world was through the use of a fable about a town called Arrowland.

An arrow is an appropriate symbol of a zinger. When someone hurts another, it is like being pierced with an arrow. It is the point of the arrow that sticks and causes us pain. It is quite apparent that when someone shoots an arrow at you, it generally has much more to do with the archer than with the target. The key is to understand that while it's the point of the arrow that hurts us, we need to focus on the feathers. The feathers point to where the pain is coming from, the shooter.

Unfortunately, arrow shooting is not a zero sum game. Some people are not as good at attacking back and instead keep the pain bottled up inside, which perpetuates behavior that is just as devastating. Arrows are sometimes internalized and the point is magnified by our insecurities, causing the target to feel more pain than was ever intended (if pain was intended at all). Often times sending one arrow results in arrows flying all over home, workplace, playground, school or basketball court. After all, we are all under stress these days.

Well, the same is true with your own arrow collection. We get an arrow, take another one, and still another. We don't always immediately retaliate, we seem to collect them and store them, arrows of frustration, hurt, and anger. The pressure builds and builds.

Have you ever noticed how some people overreact to a seemingly minor incident? Every Tuesday at 8:00 a.m., there was a staff meeting at the New Jersey Nets. The boss was a stickler about people being on time to the meeting. One morning Denise was late for the meeting. Jim stopped the meeting and said sarcastically, "Good afternoon. I am glad you are gracing us with your presence today." Denise, normally a mild-mannered and good humored person stormed out of the meeting and slammed the door.

It appears that she exploded and overreacted! Whenever we find someone responding in such an exaggerated way, it could be a signal to us that they are at the breaking point. The scary thing is that the cash-in can be at anyone, any time.

People shoot arrows to move away from their pain. This translates to a world with a lot of pain! When we reduce some of the arrows, we reduce the amount of pain in the home, office, and life. Then it will be a much happier and more productive place to be. What would it take to get the world to send fewer arrows? Wouldn't it be great if we set up our home, and schools, and our workplace to be arrow-free environments?

The following are strategies to reduce the arrows in the world. The first step to an arrow free environment:

Strategy #1: Shoot Fewer Arrows

Commit today to shoot 10% fewer arrows than you usually hurl. How about getting members of your family, your work group, and the church group to launch fewer arrows? Just think ... if there are fewer arrows where we work, in our homes and neighborhoods, the danger of being hit by an unsuspecting arrow would be significantly diminished.

One way to consciously throw fewer arrows is to follow an old adage: Think before you speak. When you are about to confront someone, identify the desired outcome. Then, focus on the issue, not the person. Communicate in an effective way to get the outcome you want without hurting the person you are confronting.

A story that demonstrates this well is "Love and the Cabbie" in "Chicken Soup for the Soul." In this story, a man compliments his taxi driver in New York City on what a fine job he did. He also winked at a plain-looking woman and later admired the work of a construction crew. In each case, he was looking to spread the positive feelings throughout. The man recognized that there is a multiplier effect to helping others to enjoy their day. The cabbie might treat his next fare better, the woman, a schoolteacher, would treat the class to a better atmosphere, and the construction crew might give 110% through the day.

Strategy #2: Avoid Arrow Throwers

It is important to avoid arrow shooters wherever possible. These are the people who criticize, put down, insult and embarrass others. Begin to identify arrows as they occur, call them what they are and break the pattern. As the target of the archer, focus on the feathers and attempt to test for understanding of the core message, then allow the sender some time to rephrase their communication.

Strategy # 3: Fill an Empty Person

What do we live for if not to make life less difficult for each other.
— *George Elliot*

An empty person is someone who at the moment does not feel good about themselves. Often, it is the empty person who shoots arrows as a way of moving away from their own pain. We can fill an empty person by paying attention to them, providing them effective feedback, actively listening to them, focusing on their strengths, and providing them with unconditional and non-judgmental love.

Strategy #4: Engage in Stress Reducing Activities

He who does not get fun and enjoyment out of everyday ... needs to reorganize his life.
— *George Matthew Adams*

Stress is often described as the manufacturing plant of arrows. Identify those buttons that make you stressful and recognize where the stress is coming from. Discover what reduces your stress. Is it reading, mowing the lawn, shopping, e-mailing your family, baking, volunteering, playing tennis, fishing, just calling a friend who makes you laugh? Do a bit of searching to find what it is and then engage in that activity often.

Strategy #5: Use Effective Communication Skills

Begin by listening twice as much as you talk. Try clarifying before you respond. Do less shutting out and more bringing in of others. Learn to disagree on issues without attacking the person. Increase the tolerance of others' opinions since opinions are never wrong, just different.

Strategy #6: Use a Win/Win Approach

How many times have you been told to use this approach? That is because it is effective. Learn to resolve your conflicts effectively so both party's needs are being met. When blocked by someone, learn to clarify first and then walk in the other person's shoes to understand the other side's perspective.

1995 — I had gone through several interviews with NFL Films looking to become one of their youngest filmmakers. The field of competition was incredibly deep and they had three positions to fill. I made it to the final four and after I met with them and saw the remaining competition I had, I realized it was tight. These guys had been in the business longer, been better writers, went to better schools. I anxiously awaited my answer over the next few days of whether or not I had the gig. On returning home to Pittsburgh I received a call from Films and they let me know that they loved my stuff, believed in my creativity and my approach, however, they chose the other three candidates.

Answer Choice 1 : "You guys are making a huge mistake, I would have worked my ass off for you and you would have realized how valuable I can be." Click. Answer Choice 2 : "I am sorry to hear that — this has been a dream of mine and to be honest, I will work for you someday. I need you to tell me where I need to improve so that I can say that I work for NFL Films. It truly is an amazing company and I only hope that I will have the opportunity to work for you some day."

I chose 2, of course. The next day I was packing to head to Atlanta for a job interview when a phone call hits me as I am leaving. "Rob, this is Bob Ryan of NFL Films (editor in chief). After speaking with you yesterday, we thought you handled yourself with class and style and we have created a position for you. When can you start?" End of story. You never know what is around the corner, so don't misrepresent yourself. The world is small — treat it that way.

— Rob Alberino, Philadelphia Eagles

STRATEGY #7: FOCUS ON THE FEATHERS

Remember that most people fire an arrow to move away from some pain that they are experiencing. Therefore, most arrows have more to do with the pain of the sender than what the receiver did to warrant it. Focus on the feathers ... help the sender deal with the pain in a different way. Don't add motivation to the arrow causing you even more pain.

STRATEGY #8: CHECK YOUR HUMOR

You know what is funny about humor? It isn't always funny. Sometimes humor is funny to some and painful to others. Often times, humor is delivered at the expense of someone's weakness or vulnerability. That humor generally hurts. Yet we know how important humor and just plain laughter is for people's well being. So what are we to do? Well, you can always poke fun at yourself and almost always be humorous about someone's strengths and you will find yourself on fun, safe ground. Understand about attacking people's strengths instead of their weaknesses.

Don't shoot arrows and when possible, avoid arrow shooters. Unfortunately, some bosses haven't heard this one yet. Do what you can to spend the majority of your time in an arrow-free environment.

The message you deliver is much more than speaking clearly and articulately with big words that make you sound smart. The total YOU is the message being sent. Think of your presence as the use or impact on others of all five senses: sight, sound, touch, smell and taste. It is important to focus on each one of the five senses. The composite you set forth will determine your profile — as recognized by those with whom you come in contact.

SIGHT

Right or wrong, people will judge you the first time they see you. Have you ever heard the expression, "You never get a second chance to make a first impression"? In fact, it is widely accepted that people will make a decision on "you" within the first three to seven seconds they see you. This seems almost ridiculous, but it is true. It is not just a fancy suit and a nice tie that are the differentiating factors. It also includes your posture, the way you walk, and even your smile.

Walking tall will make a positive impression on those who see you. You will be perceived as more confident and in control. There are very few things a person can do as powerful as smiling. A smile is tool that should be used as often as possible. Smiling is disarming and comforting. It shows a comfort zone and a person with a smile is perceived as having more confidence. A genuine smile can often be used to get you out of a tough or awkward situation or simply to break the ice. People like to be around others who smile. It is contagious.

From the nighttime security guard, to your manager, to the waitress at lunch, it is important to look people in the eye when you are communicating. Looking someone in the eye is equally important both when speaking and listening. Eye contact conveys a message that you are self-assured, sincere, enthusiastic and honest. Poor eye contact sends different messages to different people: It could be dishonesty, aloofness, arrogance, or lack of sincerity.

Neatness equates to professionalism in the workplace. Today's office environment is more liberal than it was 15 years ago. Earrings, pony tails and goatees for men and pant suits for the women are not only acceptable, but have become commonplace. As the pendulum swings toward more liberal dress code, maintaining a professional, conservative and neat appearance will serve you well.

DRESSING THE PART

Despite your new job, apartment and insistence that you have arrived as an adult, you still look like a college kid. Before you spend your graduation money or start sizzling those credit cards, you have to figure out what to wear. Unfortunately, there is not a universal guide book on how to dress appropriately at work. A good barometer is to focus on the types of clothes worn by your boss or other successful executives at work. Imitate the types of clothes those people are wearing.

To start, you need to spend a few dollars on a solid variety of suits. If you are working in a professional environment, you are probably going to need to buy suits, shirts, socks, ties, belts and shoes. You will probably not have discretionary money when you first start your job, so you must get creative. Find an upscale shopping outlet and convince someone who knows brand names, trends and business clothes (an older sibling, friend, girlfriend, boyfriend, parent, etc.) to go with you to shop. Quality is essential. Examples of places to get brand name suits, shoes and ties for reasonable prices are Nordstrom Rack, Saks 5th Avenue, Brooks Brothers Outlet, Ralph Lauren Outlet Store, Last Call Neiman Marcus and Filene's Basement. Outlet malls seem to be cropping up all over the place and one of these stores is usually found in the collection of shops. If you are in an environment where you need a suit every day, you should start with five suits, two pairs of shoes, two belts, ten ties (if you are a male) and seven to 10 shirts or blouses.

Even at the outlets, the clothes you need are going to cost more money than you are accustomed to spending. It is time to be proactive and creative. If you are getting graduation presents, ask for gift certificates or money and put it to good use. Although far from ideal, having the right clothes is important enough to charge up your credit card. Charging is a last resort and not a habit you want to get into, but it is better than starting with the wrong clothes. If this is the case, put yourself on a budget to pay off the credit cards over the next six months.

Shopping at mainstream malls can become unnecessarily costly. As a senior in college, Eric secured his first professional work experience at a brokerage house. Working for the whopping wage of $6/hour, he was on top of the world. Wearing a suit and tie each day made him feel important and grown up. He had just received and cashed his first paycheck and had the entire $420 in his pocket. While strolling through the mall, he felt that all eyes were on him. Why wouldn't they be? He looked great. At the time, he did not recognize the difference between JC Penney and Nordstrom. Eric noticed an attractive sales representative in one of the stores, and he then decided he would purchase a suit for his girlfriend because she was starting a new job. Thank goodness for credit cards. The store was Ann Taylor and the final bill came to $460, which was about

$300 more than he was prepared to spend. His pride would not allow him to look at the price tags until the final total came in and it is the best lesson he could have learned. Retail kills. Check your pride at the door and shop smart.

My first job out of school I almost did not get because in the final interview I did not wear a suit. I only had one suit when I graduated and I did not want to wear the same one back to back (this clearly showed how stupid I was. I should have just changed the shirt to a new color and thrown on another tie but I didn't). I wore a sport coat and slacks. Fortunately they were upfront with me and told me that they were thinking about not hiring me because of my "inappropriate business attire."

My comment back to them was, "If you are not going to hire me because of clothing, then that is extremely unfortunate. You just missed out on hiring a solid young salesman because he is too poor to purchase multiple business suits!" I wound up getting the job and grew their business in the Southern California territory by 25% the first year. The moral of the story is you better damn well wear a suit to all interviews even if it the same one…just change the shirt and tie!

— Brad Brusa, Sanford Corp

PROPER MAINTENANCE TIPS

Right or wrong, corporations want people who also look the part. Be thankful, because this is the easiest part of entering the real world. It is easy because it's something you can control. You have just spent a lot of money on new clothes, now you must keep the clothes looking professional.

TIPS TO CONSIDER:

— When you buy your shoes, ask the shoe salesperson to show you how to polish them. Most salespeople will be glad to sell you some polish and accessories. Learn how to make your shoes look like mirrors and polish them once a week.

— Buy shoe trees and place your shoes on them each night. Shoe trees will keep your shoes looking more professional and will help the shoes last longer.

— Alternate the shoes you wear each day; it will help maintain quality of the leather.

— Make sure you get your shirts dry cleaned after each time you wear them. It will cost about $1.50 a shirt. Request low starch to keep the shirt looking pressed throughout the day.

— Get your suits dry cleaned after the suit is worn five or six times.

— Keep an extra shirt, tie and/or panty hose in the office in case there is a mishap.

FASHION FAUX PAS

- Not wearing a belt.

- Mismatching the belt color with your shoe color. In other words, if you wear black shoes, you must wear a black belt, if you have brown shoes, wear a brown belt.

- Blue socks with an olive suit. Trust me, this will result in jabs and pokes in the office.

- Wearing a belt with suspenders.

- Wearing a double-breasted suit with a button collar shirt.

- Forgetting stays in the collars causing the collar of the shirt to flip up. Stays are plastic tabs that are inserted into the collar of the shirt. They come with the shirts, but occasionally have to be replaced. They can be bought in most men's stores.

- Not wearing a plain white T-shirt. Logos do show through dress shirts and it looks ridiculous.

- No matter how hot it gets, short sleeve dress shirts do not make the grade.

- Patches on the sleeves will come back when the 8-track player does.

- Fishnet stockings.

- Five-inch spike heels. One inch is the recommended level.

- Ally McBeal-length skirts.

- Gaudy, big and showy jewelry.

These are widely accepted principles. There are some companies such as advertising agencies and high tech start-ups where all these rules are out the window. However, no matter how freely dressed the co-workers are, play it more conservatively the first few months until you understand the boundaries.

SOUND

Take some time to observe others speaking in different situations. Go to a local high school and just listen to the dialogue in the cafeteria or courtyard. Then head over to the campus at a local college and listen to the students communicate with each other in the campus center and a professor in class. Turn on the television and watch "Larry King Live" on CNN. Watch "60 Minutes" on CBS and listen to Mike Wallace interview prominent business people and Andy Rooney give his commentary on the topic of the day. Last, listen to politicians at a press conferences, paying special attention to the opening address and the way the person fields and answers questions.

People speak differently in various stages of life and in different situations. Do you speak the same way to your baby brother, your mother, a professor, best friend, boyfriend or girlfriend? Probably not. It is important to recognize that the business world commands a certain professional business language. You can be assured that in the rat race it is better to sound like Larry King than a high school senior at a party.

IMPORTANCE OF RANGE

Range in communication will be a distinguishing factor throughout your career. However, it is the first couple of years on the job you will be most challenged to demonstrate this range. Early on in your career, you will be in more situations where range will be of importance. From the mailroom to the executive suite, it is important to communicate effectively.

Range in communication starts with respect. Respect everyone, not only because people will be more apt to help you if they like you, but also because it is the right thing to do. Scott had built a great rapport with the accounts payable person, Dottie, while he worked at the Nets. She was a very nice lady and had a great sense of humor. It also helped when he needed his expense check in one day so his rent check would not bounce.

Having range is also about recognizing that your total communication message should depend on who you are talking to. Become a chameleon. Adapt to different environments, people, and situations and act responsibly and respectfully.

COMMON MISCUES

If you want people to like you, ask them questions about themselves.
— *Edward Valentine Hinds*

Get over yourself. The "Me Syndrome" is boring, self-centered and a people repellent. Often times young people have the tendency to focus too much of the conversation around themselves. Be interested and you will be interesting. Allow people to finish their sentences and thoughts. Be patient and enjoy the essence of the conversation. Take a breath before answering a question and relax. Profanity is inappropriate in or around the office and co-workers. There is no upside to cursing in the office.

YOU ARE NOT IN COLLEGE ANYMORE!

Have you ever imagined what you would sound like if you were caught on tape? Try taping yourself in a conversation with your friends for a couple hours. A week later play the tape and listen to how you sound overall, your speech pattern, the way you put words together and how you answer direct questions. Consider this conversation in a corporate setting and ask yourself if it would be appropriate. Probably not.

You are not in college anymore, so stop talking like you are in the campus quad organizing the night's plans. Get rid of the campus slang. College-speak at work jumps out at co-workers and managers and can shake their confidence in you to represent them, the division, company, etc. If you are like most new entrants to the work force, you are still intent on using "yeah," "you guys" and "uh." Replace these with yes, addressing people by name and eliminating the "uh" from mid-sentence. Speak clearly and in full sentences when possible. How you say things is as important as what you say.

THANKS FOR THE THOUGHT

Go out of your way to be polite. At the risk of sounding like your parents, a simple please and thank you should be used when appropriate at work. Sounds ridiculous, doesn't it? Well, your parents were correct on this front. A well-mannered young person is more highly regarded than someone who takes things for granted.

TOUCH

Work is a place of business. Hugging, kissing and sexual touching is inappropriate during the workday. Keep your hands to yourself. Inevitably, you will be attracted to people at work. People are at their best and it is a great way to meet new people. In fact, both of the authors met their wives at work. While in the office, maintain a top level of professionalism. There are some legal rules about proper conduct in the workplace:

- No touching above the elbow.

- No massages.

- No patting on the back.

- No touching legs.

When meeting or greeting someone, always give a firm handshake. A firm handshake sets the tone for professionalism. The "wet fish shake" is never received well and connotes weakness and frailty.

There is a natural and acceptable amount of space that you should keep when you are talking to another person. Be very conscious of others' personal space. When this personal space is violated it makes people uncomfortable and uneasy. If people you are talking to continue to back up mid-sentence, you are probably too close.

SMELL

Take it easy on the cologne, after-shave, perfume, etc. If people can smell you coming around the corner, you have overdone it. There is always one person who stands out in every office for overdoing it. Do not be this person.

Some people enjoy a cup of coffee to kick start the day. Be careful that is not the only thing it is kicking. Coffee gives you bad breath. When you spend 89¢ for the cup of coffee, spend another $1 on a pack of breath mints. If you smoke, quit. But if you must smoke, be conscious of the fact that smoking leaves an offensive smell on your clothes, in your car and on your breath. Do your best to minimize the amount of cigarettes you smoke during the workday.

TASTE

Remember to use proper table manners when eating. Whether it is with co-workers, clients or suppliers, it is important to remember the rules your mother espoused all those years:

- Do not chew with your mouth open.

- Let the other person order their meal before you.

- Keep your napkin on your lap.

- Do not hold your fork like it is an ax.

- Do not chew on your ice cubes.

- Wait for everyone to be served before you start to eat.

Become familiar with a local, reasonably priced restaurant in the vicinity of your office. If possible, get to know the owner and wait staff by name. It is very impressive when taking clients and execs from work.

You Only Have One Chance To Make A First Impression

A study was done measuring the impact of first impressions relative to a sales presentation. Different people showed 100 company executives three one-hour sales presentations containing the same information and pitch delivered. The executives were asked to select the person they would buy from and the results were tabulated. The next 100 executives were shown the same presentations, but they had been cut down to 30 minutes. After tabulating the results, the conclusion was the same.

The researchers continued to pare down the study to see how quickly executives made their decision as to who they would buy from. Fifteen minutes, 10 minutes, five minutes, two minutes, one minute and the results were the same. The researchers continued the study and found that three seconds was all it took for the executives to make their decision.

People are affected by and act on the first impression. This is a clear message that first impressions need to be tended to in your life. First impressions encompass the total package: how you look, how you carry yourself, how you walk, body movements, the confidence you give off and facial expressions. Think about the great opportunity this presents. These are all things that are controllable. The implications of this study go far beyond sales and even further beyond work. This is helpful to anyone who has contact

Chapter 10

Change: Friend or Foe?

So you think you are impervious to change? Consider: 98% of every atom in your body is replaced every year — your skeleton undergoes replacement every three months — your skin, every 30 days, your stomach lining, every four days — stomach cells in contact with food — every five minutes.

— Grant M. Bright

with other people.

> When I decided to make the move from Philly to NY, I spent countless hours taking the train back and forth for interviews. Between answering ads from the "NY Times" and visiting headhunters that belittled me with typing tests, I was at the end of my rope. I decided that after eight months of rejection letters, I was going to give it until the end of the month and then I would resign to the fact that I was just meant to stay in Philadelphia and some things were not meant to be.

> On one of my last trips to NYC, I met with a headhunter who sent me to Hearst Magazines. It was the very end of the day and the streets were filled with massive puddles from the recent melting snow. I arrived at a relatively empty office space with my heels and stockings soaked with NYC street sludge and was definitely not in interview mode, so had low expectations. I met with a very nice woman who asked me a few questions, but it turned out to be more of a conversation than an interview. The majority of the conversation focused around sports as I told her about my current job with Villanova athletics and the very sports-focused house in which I grew up. Well, it turns out that she had a similar upbringing and we clicked immediately. Her father owned a sports bar in New York and was very good friends with George Steinbrenner and her husband had played professional basketball. Within 24 hours, I had a job offer and moved to NYC within the week to start working at Hearst Magazines. Sometimes, it has nothing to do with your GPA, but everything to do with personalities.

> — Julia Light, Playboy Enterprises

Who Do You Want To Be?

Who do you want to be? How do you want others to see you? What impact do you want to have on others? How do you want to be thought of? You hold the answers to these questions. Through your proactive approach to managing and maximizing the use of your five senses, you can and will create the self you are looking for.

E ffective verbal and non-verbal communication will go a long way in aiding you in your career. The one roadblock in your path might be your ability to accept, understand and react positively to change.

Change is the only true constant in today's business world. You will have to cope with change of all shapes and sizes. Bosses get fired, budgets are cut. Accepting this universal truth will help you deal with the unnecessary and destructive negative energy encountering change. The one thing you can truly count on in the workplace is change. The way you anticipate and respond to the changes in your environment will help determine the role you play in the future of the organization and the business world.

Bob Whittemore, regional vice president at ADP, delivered a very powerful talk on the topic of change. The following are excerpts from his talk:

> An example of breaking through old thought processes and barriers can be found in Chuck Yeager's historic flight of October 14, 1947, when he cracked the sound barrier and its "invisible brick wall." Some prominent scientists had hard data that the barrier was impenetrable. Not to be deterred on that historic day, Yeager launched an era of supersonic flight by attaining an airspeed of 700 miles per hour (MACH 1.06). Three weeks later, he flew an incredible 1,612 miles per hour, putting to rest the myth of an impenetrable barrier. As Yeager later noted, the real barrier wasn't in the sky, but in our knowledge and flight.

> Having broken the "sound barrier," we yet face a more imposing obstacle to progress — breaking the "human barrier" or status quo is as difficult as breaking the sound barrier was for aeronautical engineers four decades prior. Unfortunately, once certain professional barriers have been drawn, new ideas that don't fit the prevailing wisdom are often avoided or flatly discredited. New ideas and, eventually, atrophy set in.

> In order to survive in today's highly competitive world, it is essential that individuals and companies make quantum leaps in performance, change their habits, and shift their patterns. Today's marketplace has necessitated more change. Henry Ford's successful formula that "you can have any color car you want as long as it is black," is deader than a doornail. This line of thinking launched General Motors, which quickly overtook Ford as the number one car manufacturer.

The winds of change keep building. Blowing harder. Hitting more people. Reshaping all kinds of organizations and altering how they operate. Just look at what happened in this country alone during the decade of the 1980s."

• *Nearly half of all U.S. companies were restructured.*

• *More than 80,000 firms were acquired or merged.*

• *Several hundred thousand companies were downsized.*

• *At least 700,000 organizations sought bankruptcy protection in order to continue operating.*

• *More than 450,000 others failed.*

Some organizations will ride the winds of change, seizing the opportunity to go far ... very fast ... and sail past the competition. Others that are unprepared for the wind's force, and that mistakenly think their safety comes in bracing themselves against it, will find their rigidity a fatal stance. They will be shattered.

For years the Swiss watch companies, known for their precision time instruments and unparalleled craftsmanship, dominated the industry. Several of the top Swiss companies were approached by the group that had devised the technology to develop digital watches. Each one of the companies scoffed at the notion of a watch with no hands and predictably and systematically shut the door on this group. A small Japanese company named Seiko thought the idea had some merit and decided to be a catalyst for change in the watch industry. Seiko quickly gobbled up market share and profits by launching and redefining the watch industry with the digital technology.

One must never lose time in vainly regretting the past nor in complaining about the changes, which cause us discomfort, for change is the very essence of life.
— Anatole France

Most of us however, dislike change — we oppose change at all costs. Psychologists tell us that, as human beings, there are three things we fear the most:

1. Being Alone

2. Change

3. Possibility of Rejection

Studies show a wide range of feelings can be expected through change. Typically, you will see:

Denial — This is not happening to me.

Anger — Why are they doing this to me?

Bargaining — How can I get around this?

Acceptance — Time to move along.

Whittemore concluded that the reason it is so hard to get to the acceptance stage is that we have developed habits that make it difficult to change. In the words of Dennis Waitley, "Habits are like flimsy cobwebs — off-handed notions at first, that turn into steel cables designed to either strengthen or shackle your life."

Is life really changing right before your eyes? Do you see it? Can you feel it? It is happening and is interwoven through the very fabric of our society.

EVIDENCE OF CHANGE

Because things are the way they are,
things will not stay the way they are.
— *Bertolt Brecht*

Get ready because here it comes. Change is all around you and is happening right before your eyes. Most of the time you probably don't even see it, but it is there. The following are evidences of change:

Change is Fashionable. Young people have always been catalysts for change. Fashion trends over the years provide a telling example of the presence the younger generations have had effected change. The 1950s represented the pure Americana look. The family value decade directed the fashion, where you could find the clean cut All-American look. The 1960s were the radical times in the U.S. College students' "make love not war" protests directed fashion of the time. Bell-bottomed jeans, tie-dyed shirts and headbands were prevalent in this counterculture era. The 1970s brought Saturday Night

Fever and with it the big hair, unbuttoned shirts and long sideburns. The "me, myself and I" times in the 1980s represented a decade of excess. The clothes reflected this ideology where Izod and Polo logos could be found on everything from socks to suits. Counterculture predictably returned in the 1990s as the grunge movement swept across the country. Overly baggy, torn and dirty jeans, oversized shirts and anything retro became the trend.

Brokering A Changing Deal. The best, most successful and highest paid stockbrokers in the past were deemed "stock jockies." Stock jockies is a term describing people who pick stocks for a living and make money through commission paid on active trading. The more the clients traded their stocks, the more commission would be paid to the brokerage house; and therefore, the more money a stockbroker would make. Through the high flying 1980s, these stock jockies built large profitable books of business.

The art of life lies in a constant readjustment to our surroundings.
— *Okakura Kakuzo*

The brokerage business would change dramatically in the 1990s. The Internet, increase in available information, and discount brokers would change the brokerage business forever. The Internet brought E-Trade and other services that would cut the commission paid from the customer to the brokerage house from $50 to $300 per trade to $7 per trade. As mutual funds, IRAs and 401(k) plans were driving new consumers into the market, the large brokerage houses knew the change was coming. The brokerage houses directed the brokers to move toward a fee-based and consultative service and away from activity based commission. Some of the most successful stock pickers have fought the changes tooth and nail and have refused to move away from the old way. These people will be slowly phased out of the business.

Sports Marketing. Kevin Garnett, a 22-year-old NBA player, was awarded professional basketball's highest contract for a reported $125 million over six years. Kevin Brown, a 32-year-old pitcher, was signed by the Los Angeles Dodgers to a seven-year contract at a reported $110 million. The average salary for starting quarterbacks in the NFL is greater than the total average team payroll 20 years ago. The rapid rise of salaries in professional sports was not met with revenues rising at a similar rate. Therefore, the owners' risk of losing substantial amounts of money annually was becoming more and more a reality.

When the owners looked at the current team executives, most found ex-coaches, and a few public relations people operating businesses with market values increasing exponentially. The organizations began to recruit sales and marketing professionals in to the business and team sports marketing was born. Very few of the original executives were able to make the change to this new way of doing business, opening the door for a new crop of sports marketers.

Technology. E-commerce is changing the traditional business model and forcing businesses of all types to evaluate the current business and attempt to predict the role technology will play in the future. Those who do will survive and prosper. Those who do not will go the way of the pony express and die a slow death. Amazon.com burst on to the scene as a virtual seller of books capturing a large market share of the on-line book purchases. Amazon.com quickly branched into movies and music. Barnes & Noble, a traditional bricks and mortar business, was the market leader in book sales and immediately recognized the threat Amazon.com posed to its future success. Barnes & Noble got in the game and began to market and sell books over the Web to compete in the new game. Borders, another traditional superstore bookseller, has not aggressively entered this new field. Only time will tell how this race for book dominance will turn out. However, you can bet that those who embrace technology have a better chance to flourish.

LEVELS OF CHANGE ACCEPTANCE

> **He who cannot change the very fabric of his thought**
> **will never be able to change reality.**
> — *Anwar Sadat*

People react differently to change. Past experiences, schooling, parents and friends will all play a role in how you react to change. People can usually be classified into various groups that represent how they usually respond to change. Interestingly enough, reactions to change are rarely situational. An individual's reaction to change is usually consistent and predictable. Some people are more comfortable with change and therefore handle it more effectively than others. The following is a classification system to allow you to evaluate what group you currently fit into.

Resisters

These people regard the concept of status quo as the greatest thing since sliced bread. If this group ran the world, we would still be using typewriters and listening to 8-tracks, Pac Man would still be the hottest video game in the world, all movies would be in black and white, and people would be skating on the four-wheel roller skates instead of inline skates. Resisters fight all change, undermine new projects and sometimes try to rally support against the effort. Resisters can survive, but rarely prosper in organizations today.

There is too much change to be in this frame of mind and be successful.

Copers

Copers will tolerate change for the sake of not making waves. Copers are normally the followers in an organization. These people would have done great working in the 1950s, when a person worked for the same company his whole career. Copers are risk averse. This is a level up from resisters on the success food chain. Copers are not the people going out and getting a tattoo, not even appreciating the right of self-expression, but you probably would never know it. If in today's business environment you are standing still, you are actually losing ground. Others embracing change are passing you by every time you choose to merely cope, deal or accept change.

The first step toward change is acceptance. Once you accept yourself you open the door to change. That is all you have to do. Change is not something you do. It is something you allow.
— Will Garcia, patient with AIDS

Embracers

Embracers jump at the opportunity for improvement and appreciate a suggestion to make themselves or the organization better. Embracers are enthusiastic about new ideas and possibilities. Young people are often grouped in this category, often times because they do not have the experience or knowledge of "how things used to be done." Embracers take a reactive approach to change. This is the minimum level on the change acceptance scale you need to be to reach levels in an organization. When Eric first started at ADP there were only two products salespeople could sell, payroll and tax services. Five years later, there were three additional products added to the mix. If Eric chose to just focus on the first two products and ignored the additions, he would never have made President's Club each year. Eric was successful because he was excited about the opportunity to return to existing clients and upsell them new service and provide additional products.

> *A big challenge I took early in my career was a move to the Midwest, Kansas City, Mo. It was a big challenge in the fact that Michelle and I had never been there to visit, let alone live there. I was taking a new job with New York Life Asset Management in a capacity that was also new to me. Other than those factors, it was a "no brainer." So off we went. My job consisted of facilitating sales of NYLAM products through financial intermediaries (Smith Barney, Painewebber, etc). My territory was all of the scenic states*

(Kansas, Missouri, Iowa, Minnesota, Nebraska, Colorado, and Utah). At the time, the territory had generated a whopping $2 million in sales and was ranked dead last in the company.

I spent two years of my life traveling around the heartland and meeting with top producing brokers. After my second year, Michelle and I were presented with the opportunity to relocate back to Boston, which we jumped on. I felt like I had accomplished a lot in two years. Sales in year two jumped to $110 million and I was ranked fourth out of a staff of 16. The opportunity allowed Michelle and I some experiences we will never forget. (A full appreciation of small-town living, seeing the Grand Canyon and setting foot on sacred ground — Texas Stadium — arranged by a great friend of mine). We now have settled in New England and I have moved on to UBS Global Asset Management as executive director, but my current life would probably not exist if it were not for the decision to move early on.

— *Kevin Walsh, UBS Warburg*

Catalysts

**The reality is that changes are coming — they must come.
You must share in bringing them.**
— *John Hershey*

Catalysts jump start change in organizations. Catalysts look for new ideas and ways to improve upon the current setup. Catalysts take a proactive approach to change. The New Jersey Nets front office was full of resisters when Scott first started and it stifled the growth of the organization, so much so that most new ideas were frowned upon because they were new. A too-common phrase heard around the office was, "because we have always done it this way." It was not until Jon Spoelstra, a renowned creative sports marketer, was named president and COO that the tide began to turn. In Jon's first staff meeting he announced, "If it has always been done a certain way, it is probably the wrong way to do it and it needs to be addressed. We need a fresh start and some new ideas to get some life into this place."

Winds of Change

It is important to recognize that change is coming. If you can anticipate change, you will have more time to prepare yourself for the coming storm. Companies and subsequently, managers often develop identifiable patterns you will recognize. Look for changes in behavior and rhetoric to tip you off for change on the horizon.

Signs of Changes

- A big speech by the top dog in front of the organization talking of a major change in the organization is a pretty clear signal.

- Change in the mission statement or company's stated and public vision.

- An announcement of pending layoffs, cutbacks or restructuring.

- A merger, buyout or sale with another company.

- A planned and public expansion into new markets, product lines and/or businesses.

- Wide scale industry changes (regional bank mergers that took place in the 1990s).

Often times signs of pending changes will be more subtle. A sample of these signs is as follows:

- Uncommon visits into your department by top management.

- An uncharacteristically high number of closed door meetings.

- Members of the management team closing the office doors during phone calls.

- When people leave an organization and the position is not filled.

- A high number of people coming into the office for interviews.

It is essential to be acutely aware of the possibility of these changes becoming a reality. Recognizing, anticipating and preparing for the change will put you at the front of the race.

Fearing Change

There is nothing to fear except fear itself.
— *Franklin D. Roosevelt*

The cardinal sin in today's business environment is to fear change and act as if it is not happening. The reality is that business, like life, is dynamic rather than static. If you are not embracing change, you are not merely standing still, you are moving backwards. While you are moving backwards, you will be passed by others who have jumped on board and accepted the inevitable: Change makes the world go around.

I was working at First Call a couple of years out of college. I had recently been promoted to senior earnings analyst, a great title attached to a terrible operations job. I managed three junior analysts in addition to covering the insurance industry, essentially looking at numbers all day. My boss, a guy we called Phish, informed us he was on his way out. He had never really managed anyone anyway, so it really didn't affect the way we were doing things.

I instantly saw the opportunity and took over in every aspect of managing the group to provide a temporary solution. The group did great under my reign. We went through an entire earnings period without one error, the measure we used to track our group's success. That had never been done before. I was leading more than 25 people and felt great, doing everything I could to help the group.

When the day finally came and I went in to the VP's office, I was all smiles, very confident. He then informed me he was giving the job to another person. It was the worst feeling in the world. I didn't know whether to scream, cry, punch a hole in the wall or kick this guy in the head. I ended up yelling, then left the company altogether about a month later. I burned a bridge, which wasn't good.

I left to go join a basketball Web company, went from there to starting a basketball magazine, to becoming a producer and screenwriter in Hollywood. If I had gotten that job, my life would have taken turns that would have led me down a much different path. I could not be happier in my current situation and could not imagine looking at numbers all day, every day, ever again. I can't imagine that I did it at all. Look at every failure as an opportunity, but better yet, why wait for failure to try and improve your situation? Frequently evaluate and make changes. Go toward what makes you happy. Understanding there are steps to the top of any ladder and sacrifices to be made. Most times you do not need to stay in a bad situation. That goes for work or in any aspect of your life.

— Matt O'Neil, TOBI Productions

Now What?

Okay, you have identified that change is coming and now need to prepare yourself. The following is a step-by-step guide to walk you through the process of embracing change in the workplace.

Step 1

Relax. Do not let yourself get overly anxious, upset, excited or nervous. Remember that you will need a cool head and careful planning to navigate through the normally rough waters of change.

Step 2

Discovery. Learn all the facts and try to listen objectively. Take the emotion out of the equation. Emotion will cloud the picture and affect your reaction.

Step 3

Consider the Impact. Attempt to identify the impact on you and others around you. This will help you formulate a plan of action. It also often times puts things in perspective. Usually, the impact is not as great as you initially envision.

Step 4

Look for the Roadmap. For example, if there is a new technology push in the organization, there is a roadmap you need to follow to get yourself ahead of the curve. You might sign up for some computer classes, talk to friends who are comfortable with the technology and begin to focus some of your reading time in this area. It is rare that a clear roadmap will be put on a silver platter and spoon-fed to you. However, it usually does not take a rocket scientist to figure out the necessary steps.

Step 5

Look for Opportunity. There is a silver lining in every cloud. Change brings opportunity. It is your job to figure out where your opportunity is and prepare yourself for it.

Step 6

Jump on Board. Major changes within an organization today require leaders to get people throughout the organization to want to do what they need them to do. Often the measure of a leader's commitment can be calculated by the time she spends in support of the change, the resources committed and how she holds people accountable for their

Chapter 11

Now What?

Knowing it ain't the same as doing it.

— Old Proverb

actions. Management will appreciate people who jump on board with new initiatives and embrace new ideas.

STEP 7

Scream While Jumping. Well, maybe it is not best to scream. It is essential to let people know you have jumped on board. Tell your boss, peers, assistants, the wall or anyone else who will listen.

STEP 8

Be Part of the Solution.

> **The great end in life is not knowledge, but action.**
> — *Thomas Huxley*

Find out what you need to do to help the cause and start doing it. Generally people will be asked to change their patterns of behavior to support the transition. If you are not told, ask. Ask for clarity on what is expected of you. Make the transition as smooth as you can for others. Help others adjust and make the necessary changes.

STEP 9

Smile. A smile goes a long way. If the change is dramatic and affecting a lot of people, it will be very difficult for a lot of people. Make a conscious effort to smile through the process. A smile lets people know that you are not rattled by the change and can handle the situation. It is also disarming in a time of tension.

STEP 10

Enjoy the Ride. It might be bumpy at times, but enjoy the learning experience.

Change is inevitable. How you think and react to change as you come upon it will play a large role in your future in the business world. Instead of trying to hang on to the past, grab hold of the future and take comfort in the fact that today is the past that someone in the future is longing to go back to.

> **Remember that overnight success usually takes about 15 years.**
> — *More of Life's Little Instructions*

F antasy Land to the Rat Race" was written to provide a real guide through the early years of your career. Expect the unexpected and be prepared to deal with all of your twists, turns and challenges that will push you to the limit and test your composure, perseverance and patience.

The key to a successful career is how you plan, prepare and react to these situations.

The real life stories you have read are from ordinary people who have achieved a desired level of achievement and success and were willing to share their stories: some good, some bad; some funny, some not so funny. However, all were included to prove that your destiny and level of success you choose to achieve in the work world is in your control. None of the great business people of our time — Jack Welch, Jeff Bezos, or Bill Gates — waited for another's helping hand or "luck."

No Risk, No Reward

There is risk in this approach. You will make mistakes. You might pick the wrong job, wrong boss, wrong mentor and possibly even the wrong career. Do you pack it in or give up? No. Everyone makes mistakes — the key is to recover and get back on the right track as quickly as possible.

How do you know if you made a mistake? Set up periodic check points for yourself. Weekly, monthly, quarterly and yearly checks should be a part of your routine. Use this book as a guideline and occasionally go back and review the chapters in order to check yourself and your situation. Talk to your friends and co-workers and ask them how they see you and the career path you have chosen.

Are you happy? Are you achieving everything you want to achieve at work? Are you heading down the right path? If the answer to any of these questions is no, re-evaluate and decide how to change your behavior to get the desired results.

Winning the Lottery

Unfortunately, this probably isn't going to happen to you.

There is no magic way, easy path or four leaf clover that will ensure success in business. Successful people make their luck, they do not wait for it to fall into their laps. Plan properly, execute, follow through, evaluate, readjust and repeat the process. You control your destiny. Success is not a fluke — make your luck.

10-9-8-7-6-5-4-3-2-1 — Blast Off

Success is not rocket science. Follow the steps in the book. Commit to taking charge of your career and you will achieve your goals.

My Way or the Highway?

There is no single path to success. People are all different — backgrounds, experiences, communication styles, goals and dreams. Therefore, your path to the promised land needs to be custom tailored to you. "Fantasy Land to the Rat Race" provides a guide and the tools necessary to help identify the path that is right for you.

If not Now, When?

The time is now. What are you waiting for? The only person holding you back is you.

Top Line Take-Aways

The chapters are organized into groups. Part 1 (Chapter 1) focuses on finding the job — a critical element in leading you on the right path to success. Part II (Chapters 2 and 3) concentrates on the mental part of the game. Part III (Chapters 4 and 5) extols the value of the basics — the importance of organization, prioritization and efficiency. Part IV (Chapters 6, 7, 8 and 9) challenges you to take it to the next level with upper level communications and management techniques. Part V (Chapter 10) is about thriving with change. Part VI (Chapter 11) wraps it all up and sends you on the path.

Finding The Job (Chapter 11)

To find the job, follow the 11-step process detailed in Chapter 1 and below:

Step 1: Read "What Color is Your Parachute?" by Richard Bowles

Step 2: Be ready — it is tough to step off the treadmill once you are on

Step 3: Commit to the process — Make finding the job a full-time job

Step 4: Identify Your Interests — You will work harder and smarter doing what you love

Step 5: Identify Top 20 Companies Where You WANT to Work

Step 6: Identify and Contact your Network — Leverage any and all contacts

Step 7: Do Your Homework — Before meeting with anyone, prepare like a final exam

Step 8: Understand Where You Add Value — Know your strengths and weaknesses

Step 9: Identify What The Interviewer is Looking For — Stand out from the crowd

Step 10: Be Creative in your Follow-up

Step 11: When All Else Fails, get an internship in the desired company, industry, etc.

THE MENTAL ASPECT OF THE GAME (CHAPTERS 2 & 3)

The mental aspect of the game includes: 1. Maintaining the proper attitude, and 2. Playing the game. Use positive and proactive attitude to your advantage. Smile more, make work fun and be courteous — those are easy. Also, act as though every word and every action is being judged by those around you (including your boss).

Play the game, but do not be a poser. Use common sense to make the right decisions about the clothes you wear, the way you talk and the hours you work. It is also important to be a good protégé and be coachable. This will help identify and keep the confidence of a mentor in your industry.

ORGANIZING, PRIORITIZING & EFFICIENCY (CHAPTERS 4 & 5)

Focusing on organization will be easy for some and more difficult for others, but equally important to all. Plan, prioritize and keep a database of contacts and buy the tools (Franklin Planner, Palm Pilot, Rolodex, etc.) to help keep you on time for meetings and organized in your personal and professional life. It is also important to create and keep filing and organization systems to keep everything at your fingertips.

Set goals and aim high. Write these goals on paper and keep them visible in multiple places. Create an action plan and commit to achieving the goal. Set periodic evaluation times and reward yourself for achieving your goals. Then raise the bar.

TAKING IT TO THE NEXT LEVEL (CHAPTERS 6, 7, 8 & 9)

These chapters focus on the steps it takes to get you to the next level through proper use of feedback, projecting confidence, managing your boss and communication. Learn to give and receive feedback like a pro, it will provide you valuable information on what you are doing well and where you need improvement. The steps for receiving feedback are below:

Step 1: Remember the feedback is about you

Step 2: Listen actively

Step 3: Test for understanding, clarify and make sure you understand the message

Step 4: Help the sender, make it easy on the person delivering the message

Step 5: Acknowledge what you hear

Step 6: Thank the sender

Step 7: Review your intentions

Step 8: Decide if you want to take action to address the feedback

It is important to convey confidence in the workplace. There are some things you can do to look confident: walk tall, make eye contact when you are speaking with others, laugh at yourself, be humble, do not get defensive, and relax and be comfortable. You will be surprised at how people respond to you.

Managing your boss is a delicate and complicated task. Some keys to remember when preparing to manage your boss:

- Find out what makes your boss tick

- Get some quality time with your boss

- Respect your boss and his/her time

- Solicit feedback

Proper communication is important to earning respect in the workplace. It is important to understand that communication encompasses all forms of signals — sound, sight, touch and will all affect the way you are perceived.

If you Want to be a Player (Chapter 10)

If you want to advance in your career, you have to always be not only looking ahead, but acting ahead. What do we mean by this? We mean figure out what job you want and start doing it. You still have to do the job that's on your current business card, but start doing the job you want next in addition to that one.

> I started out as a young research scientist after I finished graduate school. My job was to work in a lab all day, inventing stuff. What I really wanted to do, though, was commercialize a product and run the group. So, I just started doing that. While paying homage to the standard R&D department chain of command, I subtly also started going around it and building my own relationships with senior business unit managers. Pretty soon, I was doing the job of a senior R&D manager, except my business card still said "research scientist." I went to my boss's boss and said, "I want to be promoted to be an R&D manager." It was easy for him to say yes because it was clear that I was already doing that job.
>
> — Bruce Robertson, GIV Venture Partners

> I tell my young people two things whenever I hire them. One, you are part of this organization — not the bottom — not the top. Just an integral part of the wheel. If you feel like you are the bottom, you will fail. When you become a bigger player and realize your worth in its entirety, look upon the next young person with the same light. Two, it is a war of attrition out there. There is money to be made, glory to be had. Realize though, that there are 100 (maybe 1,000) people with their eyes on the prize. It is a race — whoever outlasts the other will win. So trade learning for dollars, trade social life for experience — do whatever it takes to win that race. Others will drop out and go back to school simply because they are unsure of what to do — some will retire to another field because they can't live on $18,000 a year and eat macaroni and cheese — others just lack vision and self-confidence. Have all of the tools it takes to do a job, but have patience and perseverance. Those two things along with common sense and the

ability to learn and be open will create who you are.

— *Robert Alberino, Philadelphia Eagles*

The inevitable and unarguable truth is that you will face change early and often in your career. It is essential to anticipate and embrace change. There will be signs and it is up to you to identify the changes and prepare yourself for the coming storm.

WRAP

Your career is in your hands. It does not happen by itself. You need to make it happen. Good luck!

N O T E S

7411098R00106

Made in the USA
San Bernardino, CA
04 January 2014